A Year
and a Day

BOOK TWO: SPRING

Jamie P. Barker

Written by Jamie P. Barker
Designed by Simon Helyar
Edited by Jordana Ferial

ISBN   978-1517430054
Printed by CreateSpace, An Amazon.com Company

First Edition

For Jamie and Simon

Contents

SPRING

1

Defcon 3

It's *foggier* than ever today, much foggier than yesterday and yesterday it was foggy as Hell. This is unprecedented as Enrique *nearly* managed to call it in our emergency briefing this morning. The shop's full of customers and they're losing their calm. I'm supposed to be checking the weather instead of doing this. Enrique's trying to calm them out there but... If the fog lifts by noon then the plane *could* land, if not then that's it - no papers for two days on the trot. Chinatown.

It's been a great week as well. I've loved clowning around in the shop. Having said that Paula's having a bad day. She was cryi-

Hang on, I better get back out there. I just heard something smash. I'll check the weather first. Oh Christ, this doesn't look good.

Forecast for Jersey from 9am until 6pm today Friday 24 May.

Weather : Mist or fog, perhaps thinning or lifting at times. Occasional drizzle.

Max : 11 °C

Visibility : Poor or very poor, locally moderate at times.

Wind : West light F2 to 3.

Open Sea State : Slight with a swell.

Forecast from 6pm until 6am tomorrow Saturday.

Weather : Mist or fog and a risk of drizzle.

Min : 13 °C

`Wind : Westerly light F2 to 3.`

Perhaps thinning? Well some hope at least, I guess.

It was obvious there was going to be trouble as soon as I got to work. There were a couple of people waiting for the shop to open which is unusual and as I arrived they asked me about the papers and the worst thing was they had hope in their eyes. "Doesn't look good," I told them honestly. "Oh for fuck's sake!" a man screamed but instead of going home they stayed in the car park. It seemed they wanted answers. Answers I didn't have.

I entered and was met by a grim faced Enrique. "S'gonna be bad, man!" He said. He too could feel the storm brewing. I opened the shop and by this time there were more people waiting. They silently filed into the shop, most of them with their hands deep in their pockets. They milled around near the magazine rack but they had no interest in the magazines, they were interested in the empty shelf at the bottom that should have been full of the daily national newspapers.

Jersey is made up of twelve separate parishes. There's St Helier which is the capital and has a KFC, St Brelade - that's where I live as it's the best bit then there's St Clements, Giant Crow, St Adolf, St Saviour, Cat's Cross etc.

Our shop in St Ouen. The parish consists of mainly sand dunes, German bunkers, farms and a windmill and the people who live here are serious.

Paula came in 20 minutes late, her eyes were red. She had been crying or sniffing glue. I left her behind the counter and went into Enrique's office and found him pacing with his hands behind his back.

"Two day of fuckin' fog, man! S'unprecedentden-ted." He turned and paced back, "we should close the store, man! Jus' close. Fuck it" He was shaking his head. He was the boss and what ever decision he came to I would back him 100%.

"Close?" I said.

Enrique stopped and leant on his desk, his palms flat and his head hanging. After a pause he looked up, "no, we can't close."

"No, of course not."

"But we gotta get dem out of here, man! Dey stinkin' up de place."

"If we had a Slush Pup-"

"No! I want dem out!"

"I'll do it, boss," I told him. Enrique looked into my eyes and blew his cheeks out. He didn't look convinced.

"Try chor best, man," he said standing straight. "And try an' get dem to buy some Turkish Deligh."

We've got loads of bars of Cadbury's Turkish Delight. Massive bars for 50p but it's just not moving. Enrique said we could take it ourselves but it's horrible.

I left the office and pushed my way through the now large crowd to the counter. Paula was really crying so I told her to go and compose herself. Out of the window the fog was thicker than ever – so much for thinning - and I could see only half the car park. I faced the masses. I'm not great at public speaking but I had no choice. "People!" I said too quietly and so then I shouted it. "PEOPLE!" They all turned to me. "The papers aren't coming," I said and tried to meet as many eyes as I could. "It's nobody's fault. Force majuere," I held my hands out.

From somewhere in the crowd somebody, a shrill man, the man who had screamed outside screamed, "It's Richard Hammond's Motoring News Round-Up today! In The Mirror!"

"I'm sorry," I said to the part of the crowd from where the voice had arisen. There were angry mutters. A munter at the front explained she was collecting tokens from The Mail for a Peppa Pig book or something.

"And what can I do about that?" I asked her.

"You... you must have a boat!" She stammered and was greeted with sounds of applause and approval. Emboldened she continued, "yes, Spar *must* have a boat, surely to goodness! Fog doesn't stop boats!" I could hear people in the crowd babbling excitedly to each other, 'yes, a boat!'

"Spar doesn't have a boat," I said crushing their optimism.

"Well that's shit!" Said the woman. I nodded and tilted my head as if to say it was shit but it wasn't really.

"If you all leave the shop now-"

I was interrupted with a cry of, "what if the papers come in when we've gone?"

"Look at the sky! Look at how low it is, that's not going to happen, but if you leave now you can have *two* of these for fifty pence." I held up a big bar of Turkish Delight. Then I picked up a second and waved them. "Fifty pence for both of them!" At this a stout man pushed his way through the crowd to the counter. His face was red.

"Can I have four for a pound?"

"Yes," I replied and then to the crowd, "but when they're gone they're gone."

He produced his wallet, a velcro sealed affair, and brought out a pound. He nervously handed me the money. I'm sure he thought it was a practical joke.

"He's getting four!" I said waving a bar to the throng. "But he has to take them straight home."

The man held aloft his four bars as if they were the spoils of war and then left the shop. I watched him go feeling pretty good about myself. I'd gotten rid of a customer and four bars of Turkish Delight. The man disappeared into the fog and I was about to try and sell more chocolate when the air was filled with screams from where I'd lost sight of him. We all stared out into the car park, our ears tensed but there were no more sounds.

Paula though. The reason she was so upset was that she had been filmed by Channel TV while shopping in town earlier in the week. We all get filmed quite a lot over here as there aren't many people. Anyway, Paula had been filmed and then each evening she had watched Channel Report to see herself as she wasn't sure when she'd be on or why. She was on last night. She said they were just filming her and her friend walking down King Street so they'd been walking like movie stars, really strutting. She thought she was being filmed for a story on the economy but it turned out it was actually a story on obesity. Poor Paula and her friend. They were in the footage you see about fatness news stories when they just film the torsos and not the faces to avoid embarrassment, which would be fine if you can't recognise people from their flabby torsos, but you can.

2

Stalking

Going to 'stalk' Gertrude the Whore this week. Stalk, man! That makes me sound crazy. I don't mean stalk in the traditional sense, I'm just going to hang around her house, covertly monitor her movements, perhaps do a few things that could be 'perceived' as being threatening so that she will be happy to see me when I do eventually reveal myself like a white knight in shining armour and soon after she'll die (natural causes) and I'll be on easy street.

Told Enrique my intentions and he's all for it.

He whistled and said, "sweet plan, man." Enrique's a man of the world. He knows the score. "Chu could leave hav shepherd's pie a bag on her door," he suggested.

"Do what?" I asked, amused and confused.

"Chu know, shepherd's pie?"

"Why would I do that?" I asked. He looked at me, trying to ascertain if we were singing from the same music book of lyrics. We weren't.

"Meecemeeeet and potates. Scary"

"I know what a shepherd's pie is." I also know what a cottage pie is and the difference. One is lamb and one's not.

"S' fucked up, man. Shepherd's pie!" Enrique was convinced he'd had a great idea. "No complete, Only hav."

"Well, I suppose..." I looked at him. *A shepherd's pie?* "But..." *What the fuck?* "I just want to see if she has any other people visit her, you know? If family visit her then it's over. A dickhead son or something. She doesn't look like she has family."

"I watch chor wife," said Enrique, I think he thought I'd be flattered when in reality I just didn't care.

"Look, but don't touch!" I told him because it fitted the situation.

"Oh no, man. Don' fuck wid anudda man's woman," he said suddenly very earnest.

"Them's the rules."

"Jerking off s'okay. Dat h'okay," he added looking off to the side, nodding, his mouth down-turned. He was clearly thinking about masturbating. "Pretty lady," he added while smoothing down his moustache.

"Not sure," I said. I looked at him for a while longer, to see if he'd start laughing and say, 'gotcha' but he didn't.

After a few seconds he slapped me on the arm and said, 'work!' He looked like he was going to head down the confectionery aisle but then seemed to think better of it and just went into his office. I was sort of sorry I'd started talking to Enrique but now that I'd vocalised my plans it would spur me on to see them through.

Going to change my normal running routes first. I'll run past her house. Nothing odd about a runner running past a house.

Gertrude the Whore is so called because during the WWII the Channel Islands were occupied by the Nazis. Apparently back then Gertrude was a whore.

3

Fucking Kids

I ran past Gertude's house tonight in my Asic Gel Tarthers which are green and white. I also wore a green and white vest. It was a bit too matchy-matchy, now that I think about it. I just went steady. Passing Gertrude's house I saw some fucking kids had covered her front wall in swastikas and that's out of order, whatever her war crimes were *nobody* deserves that. The war was ages ago. But it also could be my opportunity.

I own a pressure washer. I love pressure washing, it's my favourite thing. Often think about leaving Spar and setting up a business where I pressure wash the fuck out of shit. Can't look at a building or pavement without thinking about how much better it would look pressure washed.

This is what I'm thinking. Next time she's in the shop I'll tell her I'll come and pressure wash the swastikas off her wall. Not actually sure it'll take off spray paint but I'll give it a jolly good go.

4

Shepherd's Pie

Gone ten last night I was looking out of our bedroom window at the ferry going past. I know nobody on board could see me without a very powerful telescope but I still smile. When the wind is in the right direction you can hear the engines. I couldn't hear the engines but as I gazed out could see my wife cross the garden which was lit only by the light from the kitchen window. She was carrying a plastic bag. Unusual behaviour. I watched as she went to the garage's side door. I was a bit worried she was going to go in and have sex with Enrique but moments later she reappeared without the bag. She paused to pick up one of her model meerkats that had fallen over. I went to bed. An hour later she came to bed. When she was comfy I told her I'd forgotten to do something and got up.

"What?" She asked.

"I've just got to check the erm," I said, I'd think of the rest of the lie while I was out.

I didn't use the light in the kitchen and quietly opened the back door and snuck across the garden to the side door of the garage, the one with the bag hanging on its handle. I felt the shape of it then opened it and sniffed. It was the uneaten half of the Iceland lasagne the kids had had for tea. I tripped over the meerkat on the way back, but quietly.

"What did you do?" Asked my wife when I was back in bed.

"I was just checking the battery charger was on." Fucking *brilliant* lie. We've got battery chargers all over the house. I knew she wouldn't care what battery I was talking about.

I'll break it to her soon that Enrique thinks food left on his door is some voodoo shit.

5

I Love It When Your Plan Gets Stolen By Your Colombian Boss Who Is A Total Fucking Dick

I hadn't seen Gertrude all week despite running past her house three times. I decided not to 'menace' her as the graffiti on her wall was bad enough. I hoped she'd come in today.

"Hope Gertrude comes in today!" I told Enrique this morning. He was reading The Racing Post. He nodded but didn't seem to be paying much attention. I thought he was looking at horse pictures and thinking about horses but he folded the paper and put it under his arm and came over.

"I've been thinin' about what chu say," said Enrique. "Chor plan."

"I went past her house a couple of times, running. No sign of family *whatsoever*," I did a smug face. "Just her car." Enrique nodded. "It's a fucking big house," I added. It is a fucking big house. Even if most of the contents are shit there has to be a few valuable bits. And the house itself must be worth loads but I'd probably live in it.

"So here is what I think," said Enrique, he looked out of the window. "I think that I should become a, er, a friend of Gertrude and then... she alone... she die, old woman, and I think I can have her house and tings."

I scratched my head just above my ear.

"Yeah, that's what *I'm* going to do, right?" Maybe I was misunderstanding Enrique's shit English.

"I think that I will do it," said Enrique. He was staring out of the window. I studied his profile. It had a moustache on it.

"What do you mean *exactly*?" I asked Enrique. There were lines crossed somewhere.

"Look at that mulaka!" Said Enrique. He was looking at Marcel in the car park. Marcel had dropped a bag of coal and it had burst.

"But what do you mean? I mean... What do you mean?" I said those last four words as one.

"S'cool, man." Said Enrique but I don't know what he was thinking about. He took one last look at Marcel, shook his head then turned, hit me with his paper and said, "work!"

I still thought maybe I'd misunderstood and he was just telling me *my* plan rather than stealing it. Then at about 11am Gertrude the Whore came in. I became very nervous when I saw her and I wasn't expecting that.

"Morning!" I said as she passed the counter. She didn't say anything. Next minute, as if by magic, the fucking greasy shopkeeper appeared. The cat food is near his door. Without thinking, there was no time to think, I left the counter and headed over. Enrique saw me coming and made sure he got to Gertude first. *Oh you fucking bastard*, I thought.

"Good morning to you!" I heard Enrique say before he looked over his shoulder at the oncoming me.

"I've already said that," I told him. "Excuse me, may I help you with your cat-food like I did last time?" I asked, even though I couldn't see her through Enrique.

"S'okay, s'okay," said Enrique shifting sideways in the aisle so his back blocked my path. "I got it," he said waving dismissively over his shoulder. He looked to see if I was still there. "Customer!" He said pointing to the counter, his eyes wide. I looked and there was a fucking customer at the counter. I sighed and headed back.

"What?" I asked the customer. The customer had a massive head. They said something about some magazine they'd ordered. One of those ones with model parts. That meant I'd have to look under the counter and take my eyes off Enrique. Gertrude was too far up the aisle for me to see her but judging by

Enrique's back they were talking. I sighed and felt under the counter but I couldn't feel it so I sighed louder and then looked under the counter. There was only one magazine with a model part on it. I brought it out. "This it?" I asked holding it up to the big headed man.

"That's it," he replied. "What's the damage?"

I sighed, *he must've fucking bought them before, you don't just buy one part of The Ark Royal or whatever the fuck it was. He should know the price.* I searched the cover for the price, shaking my head the whole time because this actually was a massive inconvenience. "£7.99," I said leaving my finger pointing at the price and looking back at Enrique. They hadn't moved. "£7.99!" I repeated about two seconds later when the man still hadn't produced £7.99. In fact he was only just getting his wallet out.

"Why didn't you have that ready?" I asked. I couldn't believe it. He mumbled something about not knowing if we had it. "There was every chance though, right? I mean *you* ordered it. You *wanted* us to have it." He eventually got his card in the reader. Unbelievable. The machine approved his transaction pretty quickly so that was one thing.

I left the counter before the customer did.

And there was laughter coming from the cat-food, Enrique had only gone and made Gertrude laugh. Had to think quick. I went back to the counter and picked up the phone.

"Enrique! Your rabbi's on the phone, says it's urgent." He looked over at me and I waved the phone, "wants to talk to you about you going to the synagogue too much!"

"Who?" Asked Enrique, the stupid twat.

"Your rabbi. Rabbi... Rosenthal."

"For me?"

"Yeah, he reckons you've become *too* Jewish? He can't handle it."

"For me?"

"Yes!" I could have said anything. Enrique was out of his depth. Enrique turned to say something to Gertrude but she had gone. I saw she was near the sausage rolls.

"I take it in de office," said Enrique. *You fucking do that*, I thought. When he'd gone in I beckoned Gertrude.

"He's gone, quick!" I told her. She hurried to me.

"They're *everywhere*," she told me.

"It's amazing," I agreed. She put her cat food and rum on the counter. "Hey, I saw some kids had sprayed graffiti on your front wall."

"Really? My front wall?" She looked shocked. Good.

"I'm afraid so, but listen, I've got a pressure washer and honestly I enjoy using it. I could come down take care of it no problem." I raised my eyebrows.

"Oh no," said Gertrude being polite.

"Really?" I leant over the counter. "Thing is they've painted swastikas."

"Swastikas?"

"I'm afraid so," I said with a sad nod.

"I did those," Said Gertrude the Whore.

"Oh! Oh right," I said. "So you want to keep them?"

"Of course."

"Makes sense."

Gertrude paid for her things with her lovely big fat credit card. "Well, anything else need power washing? Or fixing?"

"No thank you."

"Well, you know where I am," I told her. She nodded. "Let me carry that!" I told her and she didn't protest this time. We were friends. As I was leaving the counter Enrique came out of his office.

"Stay back!" Said Gertrude

"Wha?" Asked a very confused Enrique.

"Enrique, pop quiz, swastikas, good or bad?" I asked. His eyes darted around the shop like he was looking for the answer. Like the answer would be written on one of the shelves.

"Good?" He replied.

"Lucky guess," I told Gertrude and walked her to her car laughing.

6

Women

I ran past Gertrude's house last evening and she was in the garden digging a hole - looking for a mole or planting a tree I do not know. I slowed and shouted out a fake surprised hello.

"Fuck off!" She screamed, dropping the shovel and lolloping as only a 90 year-old can towards her swastikery wall. I sped up again. I doubt she recognised me out of my work clothing. I'm never going to get in that house at this rate. I completed that run at an average pace 6:21/mile but before I saw Gertrude I was hovering around 6min/mile. She really put me off my stride. Got a race coming up on Sunday so my pace - or lack of - was disheartening. I'm pretty disheartened.

I was still sore about Enrique trying to steal my idea but what can you do? The guy's got no self-awareness. This morning because the weather is nice he tells me to make sure the ice-cream fridge is stocked with Twisters and Maxibons. They're the ones that go first. Five minutes later I went into his office. "Enrique?"

"Si?"

"I'm thinking I should stock up the ice-cream fridge. Because of the nice weather. Bust out the Twisters and Maxibons." My face was the epitome of seriousness.

Enrique leant back on his chair, pondered my suggestion and eventually said, "h'okay!" Enrique is so fucking simple he didn't understand what I was doing. I'd wanted him to become agitated and twitchy and say, 'I tell you to do dat,' and then I could reply, 'DO YOU SEE?' That's what I wanted to say more than anything. I wanted to say to

Enrique's uncomprehending face, 'DO YOU SEE?' He didn't see. He would never see. I'd planned to repeat his orders all day but he didn't give me another one.

Later I went into his office. "Enrique?"

"Yes?"

"I'm putting your rent up." This got his attention. Instead of leaning back he leant forward.

"For real?" He asked.

"Nah," I closed the door, he pays a crazy amount of money already. If I put his rent up it'd take it over the £250 a week threshold and that would entitle him to running water. Fuck that. He uses the outside tap and a bucket.

Unable to exact revenge upon him I became disheartenededer. And then, just when I was at my lowest ebb the Gods stepped in to pull me back from the brink, and not just that, they also lifted me up. A rep for some shit had been in with Enrique. They were in his office for an hour doing God knows what. When the rep was leaving Enrique followed him to the door, right in front of the counter. Right in front of me. It was like some kind of fate.

The rep was carrying a briefcase in one hand and he also must've had his car keys in the same hand. I was watching, I saw all this *clearly*. The rep went to swap his car keys from the hand that was also carrying the briefcase to his free hand but Enrique misread this hand movement for the offer of a handshake and he put his hand out!! The rep couldn't shake his hand because now *both* the rep's hands were holding something so the rep went all flustered and started to rearrange the things he was carrying. He tried to get his keys back into the briefcase hand but he dropped his keys and they made a big jangle when they hit the floor! I was right there. The rep thought about picking up his keys, actually went halfway down, but Enrique was *still* stood there with his hand out. It was fucking *beautiful*. The smile that was initially genuine was now a grimace on the man from Bogotá's face. The rep did a fake laugh and shook Enrique's hand then picked up his keys. Jesus Christ, it was the most embarrassing spectacle I ever witnessed.

The rep left with his composure in tatters. Enrique rolled his head around his neck, nodded then looked at me.

"Nice handshake, dickhead," I said.

Enrique rubbed his nose and returned to his office.

7

OTS

I've been running a lot and at an increased intensity. I've not been giving my body time to recover and instead I've given it overtraining syndrome. I've certainly got all this shit.

> **Psychological symptoms of Overtraining Syndrome:** *Increased irritability, obstinacy, tendency to hysteria, grumbling, defiance, increased quarrelsomeness, avoidance of contact with coach and colleagues.*

Over sensitivity to criticism, or increasing indolence,
poor incentive, dullness, hallucination, anxiety,
depression, melancholy, insecurity.

Apart from the hallucinations. I don't have those but the rest is all spot on. Actually I don't know what indolence is but I do have a constant headache and chest pains. I'm just not my normal happy-go-lucky self and an unfortunate old person got both barrels in the face this morning.

The old woman attempted to buy some shopping, she probably had a list because of senility. She brought her shopping to the counter. She still had enough remaining faculties to know that's what you do with shopping. She didn't just start eating things in the shop. She even got her card out of her purse but when it came time to input her PIN she typed in only three numbers then stood back and made no attempt to input a forth. I was watching her and she only pressed three digits. I looked at her and she looked at me and my irritability increased. "Four," I said to her, disguising my rage quite well. She looked at me and I nodded. She looked confused. "Four!" I said to her not disguising my rage quite so well. Of course she must have then pressed the number four. "It's four numbers you need, yeah? Your PIN?"

"Yes, yes," she said as I pressed enter for her and her card was declined instantly. Sometimes the machine takes a while to process inputs before they're approved. I tend to think it's dependent on how much money the person has in the bank but I doubt that's true. If it takes a long time I imagine the machine's trying to scrape up enough money from that person's multiple overdrafts. I think the machine works faster for rich people. *Oh yeah, he's good for it!* The machine seems to say when it works quickly. Really it's probably all about servers and computer stuff. This old woman, though, she was fucking up her PIN so I couldn't guess how rich she might be.

"Declined," I told her. "Did you put four numbers in?" I asked her. I've pulled something in my buttock and standing is painful although it soon disappears when I run.

"Yes, four," she said.

"Well you're going to have to try that again," I told her. A queue of three was forming. We went through it again and again she only pressed three digits. "How many numbers are you pressing?" I asked, even though I knew she was only pressing three.

"Three, six-"

"No!" I shouted cutting her off and frightening her. "Don't tell me it!" I fake laughed and rolled my eyes. "Just how many numbers?"

"How many numbers?"

"Yes. How many numbers are you pressing?"

"Three, six-"

"No!" I shouted cutting her off. I sighed and raised my eyes to the people standing in line.

They didn't react although one idiot was looking at his watch like I didn't know this was taking a long time. I knew what they were thinking. I can read minds. "Can't use that till," I told them gesturing to the unused till next to me. "Logged on to this one," and then I raised my eyebrows to tell them we were all in the same boat. Paula is in England. I could have called Enrique but it wouldn't really help me. I was kinda glad she wasn't just inconveniencing me. A problem shared is better than having a problem on your own, or however that saying goes. The old woman was staring at her purse. "Your PIN. It's four numbers, yeah?"

"Four numbers?"

"Yeah, four numbers."

"Four numbers," she replied more confidently this time.

"Do you *know* those four numbers?" She didn't know those four numbers. She knew the first and second.

"Three..."

"Don't tell me them. Do *you* know them?"

She nodded.

"Okay!" I said. "Let's do this." I turned the keypad to her.

She typed in three numbers.

"Four," I said. She reached for the terminal and I placed my hand over it. "You're not just going to press four now? Because I said four, are you?" The old lady looked at me and withdrew her hand. "Listen, if you put the wrong number in now that's it, it's over, it's game over. You only get two shots, understand?" I was laying it on a bit thick - you actually get three chances - but it was going on a bit. In my peripheral vision I saw guy at the back of the queue just give up, replace his newspaper and leave. *He'd be good in war*, I thought. "Then they cancel the card and it takes ages to get a new one. You sure you want to do this?" She had to know the risks. I removed my hand and nodded.

The old woman's hand which she was nervously rubbing with the thumb of the same hand went towards the terminal and then back and she made an old woman noise and then decisively it went forward. I was watching her button presses now, the actual numbers she was pressing, as was everybody else in the queue. She pressed the four button. Somebody in the queue groaned.

"You think that's it?" I asked.

"Yes, I think so," she replied and so I pressed enter and her card was declined.

"That didn't work," I told her handing her back her card.

"Oh dear!" She said.

"Oh dear is right," I told her. "You'll have to go to the bank to sort it out."

"Oh dear," she said for the millionth time and fumbled her card back into her purse. The guy behind her leant over and handed me the stuff he wanted to buy and I started scanning it. As I scanned it I thought, *I bet she doesn't put her shopping back*, and sure enough she just removed the shopping from her canvas bag and left it in front of the till and then waddled off.

"I'll put that back, shall I?" I shouted after her. "Why do they give them cards if they can't use them?" I rhetorically asked as I served the man I was serving.

"Ah, you'll be old one day," he said.

"So?" I replied.

8

Drive

Enrique has been asking me to teach him to drive. For years he's been asking but I always make up an excuse not to. Excuses like; I don't feel like it or I don't want to or, no, I'm not going to teach you to drive - that sort of thing, but I recently had a change of heart. Shook me up a bit when I failed to run the shop and ran away to France. It's not that I now have respect for what Enrique does because I don't. I don't think he does anything. I just think he doesn't realize he's fucking things up. Work, his life etc. I knew when I fucked it up and it hurt. Ignorance is bliss, so they say.

I'm not ignorant, I'm the opposite, whatever that is, and now I seem to have empathy.

To be honest it's the pitiful sight of him leaving for work. He always leaves before me so I see him go. He gets about on a small white lady's bicycles with a basket on the front. It might even be a large child's bike. It's small and it's absolutely fucking ridiculous. He wobbles a lot as he generally rides with one hand on the bars and one on his head to keep his hat from blowing away. I think it's the fact that he doesn't seem to hate it that's the worst part of the whole sorry circus. If he'd hated it, hated getting on that bicycle, then I wouldn't have offered to teach him to drive but he just doesn't seem to mind and even Enrique deserves better than that so as he wobbled off this morning I shouted after him.

> "Enrique!" I shouted just after he'd got his balance and he managed to stop by wobbling then putting a foot down and hopping three times before coming to rest against my hedge. He wears bicycle clips to stop his white trousers from getting oily.

> "What?" He asked.

> "Watch the fucking hedge, eh?" At home I am the boss.

> "Sorry," he replied and then lined himself up to get going again.

"You want a driving lesson? Tonight?"

Enrique turned back to me and narrowed his eyes. "Chu bull-shitting me?"

"No, really. Tonight. It'll be cool."

Enrique's face that had been brown with suspicion melted into smile so broad it looked like he was taking the piss. He then fired two thumbs-up at me. He shouldn't have done that. Letting go of the bars completely caused the bicycle to topple even though he tried to brace it between his legs. He stumbled a bit but the smile never left his face. "Okay, see you in a minute," I told him and then went back inside.

When I got to work Enrique had a newspaper open and after I hung up my coat and rucksack he brought it to me. It was the previous night's Jersey Evening Post. It was open near the back because that's where the classifieds are. The cars for sale.

"I wan' a Cadillac, man," he said looking over the page.

"You're not going to find a Cadillac," he can't *still* think we're in America, surely to fuck? "Enrique, come on, you know we're not in America?" He looked at me but didn't agree or disagree. That's what he does.

"A beeeg Cadillac, that's what I wan'." He held his hands apart in case I didn't know what 'big' was.

"You won't find one over here, I can tell you that," I said scanning the page full of BMWs and Mazdas. "You want something like that," I said plonking my finger on an advert for a Ford Fiesta the way I might plonk my finger on a horse's name when we pick horses in the Grand National. We didn't do that this year. "Fiesta!" I said, "that's a party where you're from."

"Dat one," Enrique said pointing to an advert for a Cadillac, a proper one, a Fleetwood. 1973.

"Heh, would you look at that!" I said picking up the paper. "You don't want that though, won't be able to get parts for it. Cost you a *bloody* fortune."

"I get dat," Enrique said. He was nodding and totally ignoring my knowledge of motor cars. "Learn to drive first, eh?" I said, I was a bit annoyed.

"Tonigh'!"

"Yeah," but I was already regretting it. Enrique then put his hands out and made brum-brum noises and shuffled back towards his office, standing up in an invisible car. He nearly crashed into the cases of cat food that were ready to be put out. I actually thought he was going to, that he was going to crash, and I nearly shouted out a warning but with a yank of the wheel and a screech of an idiot Columbian imitating car tyres he narrowly missed them. "Look at me, Paula!" He shouted and then crashed through his office door. Paula was still in England. I looked through the rest of the classifieds and nearly shit.

Why didn't I read the paper yesterday like a normal person? I thought when I saw it. A wave of melancholy hit me like drunk driver on New Year's Eve. I wasn't even going to phone but I thought, *what the fuck, may as well.*

The phone rang three times before it was answered by a sleepy sounding woman. "Your advert in yesterday's J.E.P?"

"Yes?"

"Has it been sold? I suppose it has."

"No, it's still here."

HOLY FUCKING JESUS, I thought.

"Can I come around?" I asked. She said I could. She gave me the address and I told Enrique I was going out and that he must hold the fort. He owed me for offering to teach him to drive.

Ten minutes later I was ringing on her doorbell. The woman, who wasn't as attractive as she'd sounded on the phone, ushered me through to a room that was neither a living room nor a kitchen.

"There it is, hardly been used," she said pointing towards an empty table and I began to suspect she was mad. I laughed to show I could take a joke. The woman continued to point. I looked around the room.

"There's what?"

"Well... the pine dining table."

"Pine dining table?" I asked, not understanding.

"Yes?" She dragged out this questioning word.

"The advert said a ping ding-ding table."

"A what?"

"You know... A ping ding-ding table. The advert said." I mimed grasping the sides of a ping ding-ding table and pressing the buttons that operated the flippers which in turn would ping (I did the sound effects) the metal ball up to the bumpers which would go ding ding! As I was miming this I realised I'd possibly fucked up.

"A pinball machine?" She asked and then it fully dawned on me like waking up on New Year's Day in hospital after being hit by a drunk driver the night before.

"Yes... a ping ding-ding table!" I still held out some faint hope she also had a ping ding-ding table, perhaps in her garage, and this was all some ghastly misunderstanding.

"They're... they're not even called that." She said squinting at me.

"I suppose they're not, now that I think about it," I agreed with a sigh. I stood for a moment longer and then I nodded and left. But it is strange how your eyes can play tricks on you, showing you what you want to see.

9

Ouaisne Car Park

That's pronounced 'waynay'. It's where the car park is. The car park I took Enrique to for his first ever driving lesson. We went in my wife's C-Max because I can hardly drive the Land Rover and it wouldn't be fair to teach somebody to drive it that death trap. If Enrique learnt to drive in my Land Rover then he'd think cars didn't have brakes or go around corners. The C-Max is easier and we went to Ouaisne because it's got a massive empty car park. In the summer in the daytime it fills up because Ouaisne is a beach but it's not the summer. And it was in the evening. I still noticed two or three Scottish people sunbathing off in the distance.

Apart from having a beach Ouaisne is also famous for woolly mammoth bones. In the olden days cavemen used to chase them off the cliffs. I told Enrique about this when we arrived because it's an interesting fact.

"How they here? Sweem?" He asked but he was looking at all the buttons on the dashboard.

"No, ages ago Jersey used to be connected to mainland Europe."

"Don't remember," said Enrique. "What's dat?" He was pointing to the hazard light button.

"Hazard lights." I pressed the button with the red triangle and it blinked with a red light.

"Okay," Said Enrique. "Haze-ard lights."

"I'm talking thousands of years ago. Hundreds of thousands maybe."

"And that?"

"Heated windscreen."

"And that?"

"I don't know what that one is," I told him honestly. There's a button in the car that looks like you press it if you want the car to do a zig-zaggy skid.

"And that?"

"That's the hazard lights. You don't need any of these. You'll pick all this up along. That's the best way," I told him. "Ever driven? At all?"

Enrique told me he hadn't so I moved the car over to the far corner in case somebody else drove in and then I swapped seats with Enrique. Somewhere between him getting out of the passenger seat, walking around the car - I walked around the back and he walked around the front - and getting into the driver's seat he had put on a pair of cheap looking cycling gloves.

"Okay, so you want to get your seat and mirrors in the right place," I told him. He grasped the steering wheel hard and slowly turned to me. It was a bit creepy, like he was possessed, what with the slowly turning head and strange expression.

"Some say he drinks gasolina for breakfast

and put motor oil on pancakes. All we know is Enrique is called Enrique The Stick!" Announced Enrique, his head then slowly turned to look out of the front again.

"Heh, that's pretty good," I said. "It's the Stig." The Stig is a racing driver on a television show about cars.

"The Stick."

"The Stig."

"Stick?" He was looking around the steering wheel.

"Yeah."

"We go now?"

"Seat and mirrors, mah-fucker," I told him. Took about five minutes to get the seat right. For a while he could only stop it at the most forward or most backward point but eventually he grasped the concept that letting go of the bar caused the seat to stop where it was, then he did the mirrors.

I explained the gears and pedals and brakes and

indicators to him but he kept stalling. I told him to imagine there was an egg he didn't want to break between his foot and the accelerator. He laughed at this. "I don't h'understand heggs," he laughed but it worked. Although Enrique doesn't understand eggs he eventually got the car moving and did a lap of the car park. He did it in first gear and I grabbed the steering wheel a few times to straighten our progress. He did pretty good really. I didn't really need to grab the wheel but I did to show I was in charge. He just needed to relax more because it was like the egg I'd mentioned earlier was on the seat and he was afraid to sit on it. His arse was off the seat the whole time and his face was practically against the windscreen as he pulled on the steering wheel rather than turning it. I told him to relax and the second lap was better. On our second lap he told me he had some dragon bones back in Bogotá. I told him to just concentrate on driving.

We pogoed for a bit and I was minded of when I first learnt to drive. When I'd made the car lurch forward my father had said, "Uh oh, must have filled it up with kangaroo juice!" I'd fucking hated that. You don't joke when people are trying their best and it's going wrong. Enrique stopped the car at the end of our second lap and it stalled.

"Uh-oh, must have filled it up with kangaroo juice!" I told him. "No, that was good though!" And I meant it as when I'd been explaining the pedals and gears it had struck me just how complicated driving was. I didn't think he'd ever get the car to move but fair play to him, he had.

"Again! Again!" Cried Enrique bouncing in the seat. Lucky there wasn't an egg on it. I told him that we'd had enough for one day but we'd definitely do it again, maybe at the weekend.

"I'd like dat," said Enrique and he offered me his stupidly gloved hand which I shook then we changed seats.

Enrique was exhilarated and he babbled and laughed and told me of the experiences we had both experienced five minutes earlier.

"It change my life, man," he told me. "I get dat Cadillac for sure. When I was chung-" "Chung?"

"No h'old."

"Young."

"Yong. When I was yong-"

"Listen mate, you don't fucking want that," I told him. "I'm telling you." I tellinged him.

"Si, si," he said but he was humouring me. He wanted that car.

"Driving's cool though." I drove us home as casually and effortlessly as I could. I pressed buttons on the dashboard to demist the window that wasn't misted. I guess I just wanted to show how much better at driving I was and always would be. And pressing the buttons on the dashboard made me feel impressive, like a pilot.

"Yes! Hey, chu ever get a bit..." Enrique searched for the word. I thought he was going to say 'trapped' or 'stuck in a rut' but he surprised me. "A bit rapey?" He really rolled the 'r' for rapey. He also turned his hands into claws and shook them.

"Rapey?"

"Yeah, you know. Just... rapey," he did the Rs and the hands again. I looked at his hands and then to his face. His eyes were sparkling although he looked tired.

"Rapey?" Is that what he's saying to me?

"I get that Cadillac... It would be perfect."

"For raping?"

"I do *anything* in that."

"Yeah, not raping though, right?"

"Anything."

"Yeah, but not raping. Do you know what raping is?" I looked at Enrique again. He was nodding and lost in thought.

"I'm not teaching you to drive so you can go out... out raping," I scolded. "Did you say raping?"

"I get that Caddy, man."

We were home. I parked out front because Enrique lives in my garage but before getting out I needed to say something.

"Listen Enrique. You can't rape people," Enrique tried to interrupt me but I stopped him by saying "bah-bah-bah," and holding up a finger until I had his full attention. "You just *can't* rape people, I'm serious. And if you did - which you won't - you especially don't want to do it in a car like that, it's too noticeable. It's ridiculous."

"H'okay, we see," he said but he was wearing a mischievous expression, his eyebrows were going up and down.

"Did you say rape?" I asked. "Is that the right word?" But I couldn't think of any other similar word he could have it confused with. Reap? Bake? He must've fucked up. "I think you've fucked up because rape is very very frowned upon over here." He didn't reply just did his eyebrows faster and by fuck it got me laughing even though I didn't want to.

"Come on," I told him. "Out!"

10

Another Word
Enrique Can't Say

What's sitting outside work when I get there this morning? I'll give you a clue, it's that fucking Cadillac. What a fucking dick. What a knob. Enrique must've completely ignored me and bought it. Oh my Jesus Christ. The fucking melon.

Don't get me wrong, it's completely awesome but as I walked past it I touched it and my eyes flashed blue and with a whooshing sound I saw the future in monochrome and neon. The year 2078. Small spaceships are whizzing about overhead, the shop was not a Spar any more and was instead a silver dome covered in flashing signs advertising clean water and food pills but the car is still sat there, where the disabled bay possibly still was, with flat tyres and plants growing through the windows. What a fucking idiot. Whoosh! Back to the present.

I couldn't remember the exact price the car had been advertised but it had been a fair bit. Eight thousand pounds? Somewhere around there. Could Enrique haggle? I doubted it.

Marcel was by the coal and disposable barbecues. I looked at him and pointed my thumb towards the car. He nodded. I nodded then shook my head and went inside.

"Has he bought that?" I asked Paula who was chewing gum.

"Bought what?" She asked.

"Oh, I don't know. That big fuck-off car?"

"What car?"

"The massive black car in the disabled bay?" Paula chewed faster and thought about this question like it was something she could work out. *Don't guess,* I thought, *you either know this or you don't.* She opened her mouth and I saw the chewing gum. She was disgusting.

"Has who bought what car?" She asked.

It was weird she didn't know about the car. Apart from Enrique and Marcel she was the only one here. I would have thought Enrique would be going on about his car. Maybe he hadn't bought it after all? Maybe it was an incredible coincidence. Nah, there were no disabled people in the shop. Nobhead had definitely bought the car.

I took off my coat and went to his office, knocked and then opened the door. Enrique was sitting behind his desk motionless with his eyes screwed shut. He didn't open them and my first thought was he'd heroined himself to death on his drugs. It's long been an ambition of mine to discover a dead body but I really want to find one washed up on the beach, not sitting bolt upright at work, and I was a bit frightened, I have to admit. I approached him though, scared or not, but slowly. "Enrique?" I asked sharply.

"Ches?" He replied without opening his eyes.

"What are you doing?" I sat down across from him. He didn't reply. "What's wrong?"

Enrique slowly opened one eye, then they both shot fully open and he closed them tight again and started whining. It was fucked. "What is it? What's a matter?"

"Chu see it?" He asked and whined again.

"The car? Yeah, tell me you haven't bought -"

"No the car!"

"Then what?" I looked around his office and saw it. "The fuck is that?" I asked.

"I don' know, man!" Enrique's voice was high and shaky.

"Well, it's a squirrel. What's it doing in here?"

There was a squirrel sitting on the filing cabinet. I've never seen a squirrel sitting down. It was staring at Enrique. I got up slowly and it didn't run away. I went over to it. It looked at me as I approached, I approached leaning back in case it dive-bombed my face. It didn't attack so I squinted at it as there wasn't much more I could do. It was definitely a squirrel and it was alive and staring at Enrique.

"It's only a squirrel," I said studying it. "Enrique, it's only a squirrel." I went back and sat down. "It's only a squirrel," I told him. I looked back at it. It was only a squirrel. It seemed quite happy. "It can't hurt you!" I told Enrique. It *could* hurt him. It had claws. Probably wouldn't hurt you, is what I meant.

"Chu get it out."

"Fuck that." It might have rabies. It would definitely hurt me.

"Chu get Marcel Marcel."

"It's only a squirrel," I said and Enrique slowly opened his eyes. But then for the second time they flew full open in terror.

I looked back. "Fuck's sake it's only a squirr-" but the squirrel had gone. Enrique was screaming.

I turned back to Enrique and the squirrel was attached to his face like Alien. It wasn't moving.

I blew my cheeks out. "Erm," I then said.

Enrique was still sitting bolt upright, his hands were still on the desk but his fingers were playing some really fast classical music and he was making no attempts to detach the squirrel. His 'ahs' were muffled.

> "Okay!" I said to calm myself more than anything. I stood and reached over with my hands out, looking for the best way to grab it. Its arms? Under its arms? I touched it under its arms but it was impossibly soft and bony. There was nothing to it so I punched it in the back. I punched it gently because I was only too aware I was also punching Enrique's face. His cried rose in pitch so I punched the squirrel harder. It was like punching a pillowcase filled with twigs. The ultimate adversary.

The squirrel didn't budge and so I drew back my fist to punch it harder still but at the last minute I decided on a karate chop instead. It was hard to pull off because of the angle. Had to go for a sideways karate chop. The first one was with my palm up but that felt wrong so I repositioned myself, moving to the other side of the chair I'd been on and did one palm down. That felt much better. Enrique was still moaning so I built up force with each chop until I did one which I'd say was an eight out of a maximum of ten on a theoretical karate chop force scale. The squirrel squeaked and fell off. Enrique didn't move immediately, his hands were scrabbling on the desk, his feet were dancing and his eyes were screwed shut. Enrique's face was all still there though. He had a few drops of blood on the side of his forehead but he looked otherwise unmarked. The big fucking baby.

"It's gone!" I shouted. Enrique opened his eyes and his dancing feet gripped the floor and he pushed his chair back until he bounced of the back wall. He continued on his chair, rotating slightly until he and his chair were out from behind the desk and into the open. He leapt from his chair and stumbled across the room, only just keeping his feet. He then stood with his back against the wall. I joined him - safety in numbers - and scanned the room for the squirrel. I couldn't see it.

"Whizit?" Asked Enrique.

"I don't know," I told him. I saw that my coat was on the floor in front of the desk. I hooked it with my foot and dragged it to me. That allowed us a clear view under the desk if we bent down. I slowly bent my knees and felt for my coat, not taking my eyes from the desk. I couldn't see the squirrel. I stood up again, holding my coat.

"Der!" Shouted Enrique pointing to the opposite side of the room, the one with the filing cabinet. The squirrel was meandering towards us, getting ever closer looking like it meant business.

"Crafty bugger!" I said with wonder and fear then without thinking I threw my coat over it. If I did have time to think about it I surely would have missed, like the time I scored that cracker against Fiji. I hadn't thought then, just twatted it.

"Heh!" I said with relief but before I could stop him Enrique was repeatedly bringing the Cuban heels of his white snakeskin shoes down on the motionless lump with maximum force and muttering words I didn't understand. I heard a snapping like somebody stomping on a pillowcase filled with twigs.

"Enrique!" I cried. "That's my fucking coat!"

11

Fall Guy

At about 6pm last night Stan came into the shop. I'm pretty good at reading people and he was totally delighted to see me. He came around to my side of the counter.

> "Hey, hey, hey!" Said Stan. "Where's my guy?" I raised my eyebrows unsure of who he was referring to.

> "Me?" I asked.

"Of course you!" Said Stan shaking my arm. He shook my arm, not my hand. I didn't like that because it made my head shake a bit. Stan stood for a moment smiling at me but also looking me up and down.

"You're looking good," said Stan with disarming honesty.

"Thanks Stan," I replied. I've worked hard to achieve the emaciated state I am currently in and I don't mind people taking notice.

"You feeling good?" He asked.

"Not bad, you know, bit of a sore leg-" I was planning to go on and tell him why I thought my leg was sore, which involved talking about my foot which I think is causing me to run lopsided. Or some form of sciatica. I can talk about running to anybody but he jumped in and cut me off.

"Sore leg eh? That's interesting."

"I think it's because..." but Stan was walking away. He went into Enrique's office.

Maybe ten minutes later another guy who wasn't a customer came in. This one was older and fatter than Stan.

"Enrique?" He asked and it was then I deduced he was a cockney man from London because what he actually said was 'Enri'i. I pointed to the office. "You Jaymay?" He asked with his retarded and threatening accent.

"I am indeed," I replied slightly nervously and that's why I said 'indeed.' I don't normally talk like that but this guy was probably handy with his fists.

"'ow you feelin', cocker?"

"Erm... pretty good?"

"Narce," he replied, nodding then went into Enrique's office without another word.

I deal with fuckwits all day everyday and although it was unusual for people to ask after me like that I've long since learnt to not stress about situations I don't fully understand, better to just go with the flow.

The cockney man had a very loud and rough voice and I could hear his booming laughter though the office door. I just shook my head when I heard it and carried on doing my thing. I was due to finish at 7pm which would normally mean putting my coat on at

6:45 and leaving at 6:48 but my coat was in Enrique's office and I didn't want to go in and get it with all them in there so I prayed to God that they would be out before 7pm. I didn't want to work late. Of course God doesn't exist and so come 7pm they were still all in there with my jacket and I was well pissed off.

It was my anger at the lack of a God and these idiots in a room that really gave me the courage to get my jacket. Also my bag was in there with my lunch-box. There was no way I could just leave it.

I told Paula I was going and she said that she thought I'd gone and I asked her how could I have gone if I was still fucking stood there and she replied, "dunno." I stood for a moment, clicked my fingers a few times and then went to the office door. Normally I wouldn't knock but normally the office isn't stuffed with people and a cockney. So I knocked and then opened the door. At first I thought the room was on fire, so thick was the smoke, but I could just about make out the three people in there. Enrique and the cockney were actively smoking cigars. Stan had one smouldering in the ashtray in front of him.

"Going now," I told the room without making eye contact with any of them. I didn't need to enter the room fully to grab my stuff, I could just lean in, but the cockney spoke and my heart sank. "Cam an sit dan a minit," he garbled. What could I do? A man I didn't know was asking me to cam an sit dan a minit. I had to go an sit dan a minit. So I went over but there were no more chairs.

"Wool you'll avter stand wontcha?" So I stood there. The cockney man looked me up and down just as Stan had. Uh-oh.

"Stan tells me you've got a sore peg," the cockney man said. I nodded and considered how much I wanted to talk. Not very much.

"Yeah."

"You still doin' the rayce?"

"The race?"

"On Suuuundaaaay,"

"The running race?"

"Nah, the Gran' Nationul!" He laughed. *Great joke dickhead.* I smiled. "Of faking course the facking running rayce, wotcho fink I mean?" He erupted in laughter at this. I looked at the other two faces. Stan was smiling but Enrique was laughing with his hand over his mouth like a Japanese woman and I felt betrayed a bit. Enrique didn't even know what he was laughing at and yet he's formed an alliance with the cockney. The cockney hadn't been teaching Enrique to drive. The cockney hadn't beaten a squirrel from his face. Enrique had little red Adidas stripes on the side of his head, from where the squirrel had clung to him. *Who the fuck was the cockney anyway?* I looked at the floor. The blood from the squirrel - surprisingly little - had washed straight out of my jacket but there was still a stain on the office carpet. I stared at it. When the cockney stopped laughing he asked again, "you doin' it then?"

"Yes," I replied as I did intend to do it. For one thing it's the last in the series. The Spar Road Race Series. A series of races held over the winter at various distances. I'm particularly keen to do it on Sunday because I could actually win it overall by virtue of being the only person who's turned up for each one. I always get beaten - I haven't won a single event - but I always get beaten by a different person which is a victory for not having anything else to do.

"And your leg? That going to hold you back?" He asked.

"Weeeellll," I started, "it's generally okay when I get going, you know?" My leg normally loosens up after a bit, "but yesterday it didn't so I don't know." Yesterday I went for a run and my leg hurt the whole way. The cockney man did a really screwed-up puzzled face and so I continued to clarify it for him. "You just don't know how it's going to be until you start." I wasn't helping the cockney man understand and as unbelievable as it sounds he screwed up his puzzled face even more and also readjusted himself in his chair so his body was facing me more although his head was moving about from Stan to Enrique. "I think it'll be okay," I chortled.

The cockney man's head was shaking slowly, his face was nearly inside-out with puzzlement and he was struggling to speak. Eventually he got it out, "Fink? You *fink* it'll be okay?"

"Yes?" I replied only now wondering why he cared.

"Tell you wot. I'll have a carpet on you finking it'll be okay."

"Erm, okay?" I didn't understand what he'd said.

"You win that facking rayce on Sanday or I'll chop your facking balls off."

My eyebrows went up at this and I smiled a fixed grin. The cockney looked away disgusted and sucked on his cigar. I didn't understand.

"Listen, champ, we just wanna know if you're going to win on Sunday. See, we want to have a bit of a flutter, nothing serious."

"You want to bet on the running race?" *What's a carpet?*

"Sure," said Stan soothingly. "So we really need to know if you're going to win it."

"I'm going to try," I told him, looking into his eyes. Stan winced a bit.

"See, trying isn't good enough," said Stan apologetically. I looked at Enrique, he was just smoking and looking at the end of his cigar. He was a bit cross-eyed. "We need to know if you're going to win," Stan said, "and we need to be *certain*, you understand?"

"I can't guaran-" I began

"So what about *not* winning," said Stan chewing the end of his cigar. I could tell he was getting frustrated..

"Oh I could do that," I told him. Stan looked at the cockney, only briefly but I saw the mischievousness in his eyes.

"You could lose the race on Sunday?" Stan asked. "That's wouldn't create a... I don't know, a moral dilemma?"

"Well, I guess I'd feel a bit shit," *no I wouldn't it's my dream scenario*, "but I understand how it is. I'm a man of the world."

"We'll make it worth your while, son," said the cockney.

"That would be cool," I told him. Then the three of them just sat there nodding and sucking on their cigars. "I'll be going going then?" I said.

"Yeah, you run along," said the cockney and then he exploded into another storm of laughter at his wittiness and so I did but mine was fake.

This morning a package was delivered. The card read:

> *Friends stick to agreements. Good luck on Sunday,*
> *I'll be watching.*
> *Regards,*
> *Tony*

Inside was a full set of coloured ink cartridges for a printer I don't have.

I didn't win the race. Some fucking guy I've never even seen before in my life did.

12

I'm Not a Racist But...

I'm not a racist but I went for the panic button when I saw the black man. Just instinct. It's not my fault and if you want to blame something then blame TV. TV has conditioned me this way so at 7pm last night when the black man came in my first instinct was to push the button. Actually my first thought was, *what is this, a dream or something?* Then I went for the button. I didn't push it though, not immediately, because I'm not a racist but understand, a black man has *never* been in our shop in all the time I've been there, let alone at 7pm on a Thursday night!

The man nodded at me and I smiled back, remembering what we're taught in the Spar. If *you* get robbed it's coming out of *your* wages. You learn that Day One.

The man was looking for something. Scoping the shop out? Possibly. He was possibly just looking for something to buy - a bottle of Oasis or perhaps a packet of razors for his lovely bald head. Fucking hell, black people are cool as well as intimidating. Maybe that's why they are cool? Like Donald Trump? I wish I could rock a bald head. And they can wear *anything* and look cool as fuck. Anyway there was no way of knowing how the situation with the black man in our shop was going to play out without letting it play out. It was in the God's hands.

He was wearing a padded body warmer and really long shorts and he looked down the first aisle which leads to the bread. This guy didn't want bread, though. No fucking bread for this guy. When I wear shorts with pockets I end up looking like a scout leader, this guy didn't look like a scout leader. He looked down the next aisle. Paula was at the end second aisle. The guy headed down that aisle. Oh Jesus Christ.

"Paula!" I shouted rather weakly. She looked up just in time and I saw her dart to the side. I looked around for a weapon but there was nothing, absolutely nothing. Would he mistake a pricing gun for a tazer? Unlikely. I heard her, Paula, shout and I pressed the button and time stood still. I couldn't see either of them. Enrique came out and looked at me. I pointed down the middle aisle. There were muffled sounds coming from the proximity of the hot food counter. Enrique couldn't see down that aisle from his door and so I pointed twice more and then tilted my head that way.

Enrique did his 'Que?' face and so I pointed down the middle aisle three times really violently, my face twisted with silent emotion. Enrique took two slow steps but looking at me. I tilted my head again. He took another step but he didn't like this. He was expecting something to jump out on him wearing a mask. I went over to him.

"There's a man down there," I whispered looking down the aisle. I could hear Paula pleading with the man but couldn't get a visual. "And he's black."

"Down der?" Asked Enrique looking down the aisle I'd just looked down.

"Yes, down there, he's got Paula," I said. Enrique anointed himself with the sign of the cross. "Come on," I whispered but I meant 'you go on.' Enrique headed tentatively down the aisle. It was the confectionery aisle so there were no tins to grab. Enrique walked slowly down the aisle and I was hunched over behind him. Hiding behind a human shield really if I'm honest. I grabbed onto the back of his jacket and he didn't seem to mind. I was holding him so that he couldn't turn and peg it back passed me. I was behind and I was fucking *staying* behind. We were halfway down the aisle, both hunched over and tiptoeing when Paula appeared.

"What are you perverts doing?" She asked. The man appeared next to her. He looked at us and then to Paula. Enrique and I were stood like melting statues. "Nobheads," said Paula. Enrique looked back at me. *What are you looking at me for?* I thought, *can't you make a decision?* I didn't know what to do and so I stood up straight.

"Hello!" I said. Paula narrowed her eyes at me and shook her head.

"This is Wellington," Paula announced. "Wellington, these are the people I work with," she gestured towards us the way you might gesture towards a broken plate.

"*That's* Wellington?" I said. I hadn't seen THAT coming.

Paula's been going on about Wellington all week. She met him at a rave or church or something, last weekend. She loves him or something. She's been talking about him a lot.

"Hi!" Said Wellington, raising a palm.

"Hello!" I said exactly the same way I'd said it initially. Enrique had gone right down and was pretending to tie his shoelace. Enrique's shoes don't have shoelaces, they're slip-ons. I watched him tie his invisible shoelaces. Paula and Wellington were also watching.

"There!" Said Enrique when he'd finished and then he stood up and straightened his jacket down with three sweeps of his hands. "Good day!" He said and then turned and walked back towards the counter. He paused at the end, and went over to the front window. I know he was just checking if his RapeMobile was still there, ensuring it hadn't been stolen on this night of near anarchy. He eats his lunch in it. I'm giving him another driving lesson tomorrow. Enrique then returned intently to his office.

I turned back to Paula and Wellington. They were expecting me to speak.

"I've heard a lot about you!" I told Wellington brightly.

"All good I hope!" He said and then I laughed wildly. Oh man, he was well spoken and everything, like a children's TV black man. He was so awesome. Honestly I couldn't remember *anything* Paula had told me about Wellington. I remembered his name, of course, because it's fucked and I'd said, 'be careful he doesn't give you the boot,' a number of times but I remember *vividly* Paula not telling me Wellington was black. I remember the *exact* moment she completely failed to mention it.

When I finished laughing Wellington was kissing Paula - just a peck, nothing gross, he was a class act - and then he was going. We both watched him go. How come black people just have muscles? How's that fair? Wellington was fucking brilliant. I wanted him to be my best friend. And then he was gone.

I rotated to Paula.

"*Why?* I mean, *Jesus!* Why didn't you say he was black?" I asked her.

"Didn't I?"

"No, you *totally* didn't. I would have remembered that."

"Well, what difference does it make?"

"It *doesn't* make a difference," I told her. I keep forgetting how stupid Paula is. "But I mean, if you were going out with a fucking giant you'd mention it wouldn't you?" Paula considered this. "I mean, you go out with a giant then when you're talking about him you're going to fucking mention he's as big as a cinema? Surely to fuck? It's going to be one of the first things you say!"

"I thought I did say. It's no big deal though."

"No, of course it's not *Paula*. Fucking hell I'm not a racist but if you were going out with a guy with three heads it'd come up in conversation, surely?"

"I suppose. It just didn't seem..." Paula's sentence just petered out.

"He seems lovely though," I told her. "There's nothing wrong in what you're doing." "What do you mean?" She asked naively.

"Don't be ashamed of him."

"What?"

"Shush Paula," I told her and then I stared out of the window.

13

Natural Selection

They say you can't teach an old dog new tricks but if changing gear in a car is a new trick and Enrique's an old dog then that whole thing is bollocks because I totally taught Enrique to change gear. Fucker's picking up the whole driving thing pretty damn quick. We went back to Ouaisne car park and as well as just going around we also did some manoeuvres. Nothing too taxing, a bit of reversing and pretending to park. As he drove I had my elbow out the window. Just chilling. That's all.

It's not like I'd smuggled a puppet into the car and it was on my hand. The hand that was out the window. As if I'd do that.

Yeah, I did that!

> "What do you reckon about Wellington?" I asked Enrique. I've been thinking about Wellington a lot. He was so cool. As I spoke I slowly raised the glove puppet that was on my hand. Fuck knows what animal it was supposed to be. I'd bought it in Hamleys when I went to London when the kids were small and less bothersome. It was brown and furry. Perhaps a sloth.
>
> "He seem h'okay," grunted Enrique wrestling with the wheel, checking the position of the gear stick and staring intently at the wing mirror. He was going to make us go backwards!
>
> "He does seem pretty cool," I agreed. "Paula's done well." Enrique was making us go backwards. He was sweating. "Paula's a bit rough, eh?" I added. I was wiping the sloth slowly up the outside of the car door.
>
> > "Am I okay?" Asked Enrique.
>
> "Yeah go for it," I told him. There was nothing he

could crash into and backwards we went. "Wonder what he does, do you know what he does?" I asked Enrique. He was probably a better listener that I was. "Who?"

"Wellington."

"Lo no say," he said bringing us to a halt and applying the handbrake as I'd taught him. He exhaled. "We go around again?" He asked, licking his lips.

"Yeah, go for it," I told him. I am *rarely* in the passenger seat of a car and it was a nice change. I never let my wife drive me because she's a woman but Enrique's a man and even though he can't drive I felt safe.

"*You'll* be able to get yourself a woman soon, eh?" I said but I knew what was coming and I stifled a chuckle. We were off again and he didn't turn to me because he was concentrating on his driving but he did do his disturbing eyebrows and he made a guttural noise. "I mean a girlfriend!" I laughed.

"Pah, girlfriends. Jus' trouble."

"You don't want a girlfriend?" I asked him. I'd fucking

love to have a girlfriend. I briefly thought about Carol.

"Trooble man," Enrique countered. Enrique had obviously experienced trouble with a woman or perhaps with women and it had left an indelible mark. "Who need girlfriend?" He asked and before I could reply he said, "hey, you come home an' wife gone. Chu better..." he did a crunching gear change.

It was time.

"Fuck! Enrique look!" I shouted. With my right hand I pointed to my wing mirror. I'd raised the puppet and was holding it quite close to the mirror. "The fucking squirrel's back!" I excellently acted being very scared and then I was about to laugh when Enrique put his foot down and then I no longer needed to act.

"Fu!" I managed as the G-force threw me against the door. I managed to pull my hand in and Enrique saw the puppet. He must have thought it climbed in. He pulled the wheel to the side, the pedal still flat to the metal and we were rallying. I grasped around, trying to to find something to hold on to. Anything. I felt I was going to fall out. Enrique looked at my grasping hand and screamed and I was screaming and he was screaming and he tried to punch my hand but he wasn't slowing down and we were powersliding around the car park, a large plume of dust following us. We were dead. We were heading to the tractors. I screamed and he screamed and I tried to curl up into a ball but I was still getting pulled about. I closed my eyes. The impact didn't happened when I expected it and I felt us straighten up. I opened one eye and saw, to my amazement, that Enrique had missed the tractors and we were fishtailing it down the straight. "Brake!" I screamed, twelve octaves higher than I've ever screamed before. "Brake!" I grabbed the handbrake and pulled it as hard as I could. Any harder and it would have came off in my hand and then we were spinning.

Enrique had let go of the steering wheel and had his palms pressed against the windscreen. I was moaning now, my eyes screwed tight shut. Screaming was pointless. I couldn't hear the noises, if any, that Enrique was making. And then it was silent. I could smell heat and the blood was still lapping around my brain.

"Ha!" I said but then I was crying. Tears of relief really. I looked to Enrique but his door was opened and he was scrabbling away from the car, trying to get upright. I cried more. Proper crying face. Enrique was upright and running. He was holding his hat on with one hand to stop it blowing away.

I looked at my hand and cried harder. Then out of the windscreen at the dustcloud that was blowing out to sea. That dust cloud was poignant and I lost control. I took the puppet off my hand and started whipping it against the dashboard. It had hard eyeballs which made a cracking sound. I did this until I heard Wellington.

"You okay?" He asked. I turned slowly to the open window. Wellington was leaning over and removing earphones. I looked back at the puppet and then wiped my nose with it. I then stretched my face.

"Yup."

"You sure?"

"Yeah, fine." I stretched my face a few more times so that he might think my crying face had just been some facial exercise. "What are you doing? Running?" Wellington looked like he'd been running. He was wearing running gear.

"Just a jog," he said. He still looked concerned.

"A jog." I said. I sniffed. I was looking at the

horizon. Perfect. Wellington jogging is probably me running flat-out, and that's not being racist, that's just the way it is. Running is the only thing I'm slightly above average at. I nodded.

"You sure you're okay?" He asked. He was staring at the puppet. I looked at the puppet and then back to Wellington. I held the puppet up but could think of no words to go with that action.

"I'm fine."

"Okay," said Wellington and he put his earphones back in his ears. He looked at me a moment longer, looked like he was going to wave or something then, after checking his watch, he began jogging. I nodded. I watched him in the wing mirror. Jogging my arse, he was fucking running. I sat for a few minutes longer before getting out and going around to the driver's side. As I drove through the car park I tried to feel if the car felt broken. It did a bit but that could have been my imagination. I passed Enrique halfway up the hill and didn't slow.

14

Armour Of God

Paula came in this morning walking like she just got off a horse after an epic journey on a camel.

"What's wrong with you?" I asked her. She didn't reply. "Enrique, check out Paula, she's all pleasure bent!" I shouted merrily. Enrique came over and checked out Paula's walk.

"Holy fucking shit!" Exclaimed Enrique. Paula

made a spastic sound at him and continued her slow progress to the hot food counter. Paula moving like a 100 year-old female cowboy. We both stood and watched her and cheered her on with cries of, "go on, you bastard!" And "nearly there!" and "do it! Do it! DO IT!"

"Did he smash your back doors in?" I asked her because I didn't want to go for the obvious. Enrique sniggered. Paula replied with a very high-pitched fake laugh.

Enrique wasn't so worried about the originality of his statements. "So es true what dey say, huh?" He looked at me and nodded. I smiled but what he had said was pretty lame. Paula had made it to the counter. She held on to it for a bit to recover. Enrique is shit at being funny and he repeated himself, "es true, huh? Black men? Big cocks? Huh?" He wasn't smiling so much now but Paula did a great job at ignoring him. "Is it true? IS IT!" Demanded Enrique, the humour gone from his voice.

"Easy there, Enrique," I told him, putting a hand on his shoulder.

"Heh," responded Enrique. He had removed his handkerchief and was dabbing his face.

"So a good night then?" I said because the mood was weird. I didn't expect Paula to respond and I had begun turning back towards the front of the shop.

"I had an abortion," Paula said in a small voice. I paused, I didn't know whether to turn to face Paula or just continue to the till. I looked at Enrique.

"Woah!" He proclaimed with his hands up in front of him. He then backed away. He walked backwards all the way down the aisle and around the corner and as far as I know all the way into his office without looking where he was going. Not even once.

I decided not to turn back to Paula, she probably wanted to be alone. "Okay," I said to, well, you know, let her know everything was okay. I then went back to the till and listened to her sob. It started to fuck me off after a couple of hours.

15

Joker

I must say the very sight of him cheered me right up and, I'll be honest, I needed cheering up. Hey, Jesus Christ, will you stop fucking with me? Do that and I might start believing in you. I'll spread the word and everything, just stop. fucking. with. me. Don't know if these are trials or something but I don't respond well to trials. I respond well to positive reinforcement and specific praise. Do something nice for me. Instead of having me get up and finding my fence has blown down how about leaving a hoard of Roman coins? Something like that. I don't really care. Fuck it.

And Paula. She's still miserable so the sight of the fat chap really cheered me up. It was the way he carried his massive blobby self. I think it was his confidence that impressed me most. It's great when you see really fat people who are totally comfortable underneath all that fat.

When he came in the shop he wasn't gazing at the floor, hoping nobody would see him as he bought food he clearly wouldn't need for about three months. He wanted to be seen - that was obvious from his colourful shirt which was very colourful indeed. He wasn't trying to hide the fact that he was a big fat fuck, in fact with his outrageous attire he was actually drawing attention to it. He was great.

"Ay up," he said to me upon entering the shop. He was the kinda guy who winked at people though he didn't wink at me.

"Hello!" I replied. He headed intently to the hot food counter, no fucking about and he was singing to himself as he went. I think he was trying to click his fingers but I think his fingers were too fat or greasy to actually click but no mind, big fat people are generally great singers and this one was no exception. He blocked out Paula and half the counter when he was down there but I could tell from the way his back moved that he was pointing at multiple things. This guy deserved to be somewhere where people paid to look at him. He just gave off that vibe, he was a born Show Man.

I don't normally look at people but when he turned to me with his four paper bags I just kept right on looking and smiling. He nodded and he practically danced down the aisle towards me still singing and stopping only to pick up a packet of crisps.

"Four sausage rolls, a cheese and onion pasty and a scotch pie," he said helpfully so that I wouldn't have to look through the bag. I trusted him. Why would he lie? I rang it up and his McCoys.

"Anything else?" I asked. I don't normally ask but I liked this guy.

"You din think that's enoof?" He laughed. I laughed too.

"Why have a six pack when you can have a keg, eh?" I said.

"What?" He asked. I looked up at him and laughed. He had a grin on his face. I figured he was so fat he needed hearing aids.

"Just saying, you've got to maintain that figure."
"I'm sorry, pal, I dint understand," he said.

"Ah, nothing," I told him.

One time I was in Paris in a restaurant with my wife. Can't remember what we ate but the guy on the table next to us ate plate after plate of oysters. The waiters must have brought him ten plates of oysters. At first we didn't pay much attention to him but soon it was all we could concentrate on. Was he going to have another plate? Of course he was, surely not another! It must have been some kind of all-you-can-eat deal. When it came to oysters all, for the man who sat on the next table in that restaurant in Paris equalled, loads.

When we finished our meal the Oysterman was still going for it and paying at the till I made the mistake of saying, "that guy sure can eat oysters," to the waitress. I thought she'd laugh and go 'oui!' I said it in English as all night the staff had understood my English. Not this time though.

"Pardon?" Said the attractive lady waitress.

"I was just saying, that guy can eat oysters," I told her. She still didn't understand. I could have went over to the man who was quite near us and said, 'this man' pointing to the man. 'He eat,' doing eating actions. 'Beaucoup,' that means lots. 'Of oysters,' pointing to the oysters. I didn't do that.

"I'm sorry," she said but I could see she was genuinely sorry she couldn't understand me. She probably thought she was good at English.

"Don't worry about it," I told her.

"No, no," she said and then to my horruer, "I get somebody," and before I could stop her she'd disappeared into the kitchen to get somebody who could understand my talking. My skin was crawly and I screwed my eyes shut. I opened them to see the waitress ushering a man in a suit towards me. I think he was the boss.

"You say?" She said to me.

I took a deep breath. "I was just saying that that guy eats a lot of oysters."

"Him?" asked the man in the suit pointing at the man eating oysters. The man eating oysters looked at us. I smiled.

"Yes," I replied. Neither the man in the suit or the waitress knew what the fuck I was on about.

"It's okay." I told them both.

"Ah, okay," said the man in the suit.

We then paid and left.

The point is sometimes it better to know when to shut up so with the fat guy I decided to shut up.

> "I just... £7.62 please," I said but I was still smiling. I thought he was playing. He handed me a ten pound note. I put it in the till and gave him his change which he fumbled into his purse. Then he leant over the counter as best he could. I leant back a bit.

> "Listen ya fooking queer," he said to me quietly, "you ever fooking so much as look at me again am ganna fooking open ya up." He wasn't smiling any more.

> "I didn't... I just..." I said and the fat man left while staring at me, his double chin snagged on his shoulder when he finally faced forward. After he was gone I stood behind the counter, playing with my lower lip then I was going to go and talk to Paula. On the way I remembered she was miserable so instead I went to ask Enrique if he knows what's happened to my kayak.

> "Ye said sum'it aboot me figa?" He asked. He could hear after all, what a joker!

16

Incest

Enrique came out of his office just as I was about to enter. "Strange incest in the office, man." They were the words that Enrique used, the fucking idiot. "Come, come!" he beckoned me to follow him.

"Incest?" I asked him.

"Incest *everywhere*," he confirmed.

I couldn't be bothered. It wasn't worth it. I wasn't expecting strange incest going on in his office - a mother and her brother going at it on a trapeze, for example - and if I was feeling brighter I would have ribbed his poor English a bit. I wasn't feeling brighter. Paula's situation and being threatened had dulled my buzz. His office was a mess.

Enrique walked around pointing out the beetle things.

"Where are they from?" I asked.

"Dey *everywhere!*" Replied Enrique answering a question I hadn't asked. I mean, I hadn't asked, 'Enrique, these bugs that are everywhere, are they everywhere?' If I'd asked that then his answer would have been correct. I'd asked him *where* had the bugs come from, he must have an idea. "Everywhere! Oy, oy, oy!" He said looking around, pointing them out and shaking his head.

They were everywhere. I could see twenty, at least. They looked like mint humbugs. We both stood for a while looking around. We would have stood there all day if I hadn't offered a solution. Enrique was waiting for me to offer up a solution. "Shall I get the hoover then?" I asked. Enrique starting nodding, at first hardly noticeable and then full-on and vigorous.

"Yes, get de hoover. I think dat is best," he said and

I went to get the hoover which lives outside of the toilet. I got the hoover and heard Enrique scream. My first thought was that the squirrel was back so I rushed back to the office. Carrying the hoover is a complete fucking nightmare of cables and pipes and the dangling plug banged my shin as I went. It was only a plug but it must have got me right on the bone because it really hurt but I didn't stop to rub it. Instead I cursed Paula - abortion or no abortion - for not winding the lead back properly last time she used it.

It was probably her because I hate using the hoover but to tell the truth I was quite looking forward to hoovering up the beetles. It would be fun. Oh yeah, Enrique had screamed.

I burst back into the office. Enrique was standing behind his desk. His left hand was covering his mouth, his right hand pointing down. Of his face I could see only his eyes and they were filled with desperation. He looked up at me and then back down to whatever he was pointing at.

"What is it?" I asked still holding the hoover, but Enrique just looked up at me and down again, he couldn't talk. I dropped the hoover.

His bottom drawer, his special drawer - his heroin drawer - was crawling with bugs.

"For fuck's sake!" I said. It was like a scene from a horror film about beetles in a drawer. Along with the creepy crawlies in the drawer there was a hardback book sized package that seemed to be wrapped entirely with parcel tape. A corner was gone and the bugs were coming out or going in, it was impossible to tell for sure. There was also what looked like sand but what I knew to be heroin spilling out. "You shouldn't have that shit in here," I told him. He looked at me and back to the drawer, still pointing, still covering his mouth. Telling him he shouldn't have his drugs here was the shock at seeing the bugs talking.

Not seeing the bugs talking. The bugs didn't talk.

Seeing them made me talk that. Fuck.

I actually *make* him get it delivered to work because I won't let him get it delivered to my house. Enrique hasn't got a letterbox on my garage so any post delivered to my house has to be heroin free. When personal letters for Enrique (coloured envelopes, hand written address. From his sister. I think) get delivered at ours I hide them. I don't know why I do that, thinking about it. I've never thought about it before. I just started doing it and then I had to keep doing it.

"I'll hoover them," I told him, looking around for

a plug socket. I did the free-roaming ones first and it was satisfying, the little rattle as the tiny disgusting creatures vanished up the bendy pipe was satisfying. I felt a little bit like a Ghostbuster.

Enrique was still staring at his drawer. "Enrique!" I whisper-shouted over the noise of the suction. He looked at me. I looked around to make sure we were alone. "I could have done Paula with this!" I made a jabbing movement with the end of the hoover. Enrique dropped the hand that was covering his mouth a laughed a little and then he reverted to his previous pose. I went around getting the bugs not knowing why I'd just said that about Paula.

After only a few minutes I'd got all that I could see that were loose and I moved Enrique out of the way so I could get to Ground Zero. Now I was in the swing of it I was looking forward to tackling the drawer - it wasn't a million miles away from my second favourite activity, power washing.

I put the end of the hoover in the corner of the drawer where there was a drift of bugs, careful not to let anything substantial get sucked onto the nozzle and cause a blockage and careful not to get too close to the package and suck up his drugs although I felt we were going to have to do just that. When the drawer was empty of visible bugs, save for the ones on the package, I looked up at Enrique. I raised my eyebrows to ask, *do you want me to do this?*

He lowered his eyebrows to tell me, *only do it if there is no other way*. I shook my head to tell him, *this is the only way*. He nodded to say, *do it then, if you must*, and I put the hoover on the corner of his package. The hoover hose went mental and shook around as lumps of Enrique's hard earned heroin and horrible beetles went bye-bye.

When the package was empty and had lost its shape I squashed it by bashing it with the hoover nozzle. I stood up. Enrique clapped me on the back. "I'm sorry," I told him, surveying the drawer. I had another look around the office. Found two more bugs and hoovered them. Luckily I hadn't unplugged the hoover at the stage as plugging it back in would have been a bit of a chore.

Enrique checked out his chair before gently sitting on it.

> "You're going to have to empty that somewhere," I told him, pointing at the hoover. "They'll crawl out and get us." He nodded. He'd steepled his hands under his chin. "You'll have to do it quick," I stressed.

I then left his office. Paula was behind my counter.

> "What was that about?" She asked.

> "Nothing," I told her. "How's your fanny?" I asked.

"Fat and sassy," she replied but she still wasn't ready to smile.

"Cool."

17

Drama

I've been nice to Paula today because I'm a nice guy. But I'm *just* nice, you know? Don't need shitty gestures or anything. So I was being nice to her, talking nice to her and Enrique comes over all awkward and shuffling because of his lack of interpersonal skills.

> "Here!" He near shouted and thrust a small white teddy bear into Paula's personal space.

> "Aw, thanks," said Paula taking the bear. I recognised

it straight away. It was from the pile of small white teddy bears that we'd got in for Mother's Day. The bear, which was only about three inches tall, was holding a red heart shaped card. On the front of that card was the word 'Mummy.' "It's lovely," said Paula. Enrique gazed upon her and smiled like a foreign Jesus.

It was not lovely at all. "Enrique, what does that say on the card?"

"Mummy?" Replied Enrique.

"Well?" I asked. Enrique is so stupid and tactless it is literally amazing. "Mummy? You've given Paula a small bear holding a card that says 'Mummy'? Did you really just do that?" "I just did dat," replied Enrique.

"After what *she* did? You think that's right?"

"I er..."

"You think she wants to be reminded of it?"

"No!" Said Paula, she sounded like

she was getting upset again.

"It's okay, Paula, I'll handle this,"
I told her.

"It's just thoughtless, Enrique, you gotta *think* more
before you act." I tapped my head when I said the
word 'think'. Paula was moaning. "Paula, look at
me, you've done *nothing* wrong," I told her, and I
firmly believe that. I wasn't just saying it. How can
it be wrong to destroy something you've created?
Nobody gave her that baby, she made it. How can
it be wrong for her to kill it? If I built some shelves
and then smashed them up I wouldn't expect the
police around to arrest me. "Paula, I firmly believe
you should be able to kill your own kids," I stressed
but she was full on crying now, because of Enrique.
"Nice one, dickhead," I told him before turning back
to Paula."Up until they're five years old."I looked at
Enrique, he was gazing out of the window. "Or six.
Yours might have died on its own anyway."

"What is that?" Enrique was squinting. I looked out
of the window just in time to see the police tractor
fly past at 18mph. One could have been ignored but
then another one went past and another. Three went
past in total, all bright red with blue flashing lights
on that bit in front of the massive steering wheel.

What added more gravitas was the policemen sat atop them with determined expressions fixed upon their fearless and formidable faces.

"Something big is..." Should I say 'going down' or 'up' I asked myself. "Something big is up," I said but it didn't sound right. "Something big is going down." As I was in protective mode towards her I said, "Paula, stay here!" And rushed out into the car park. Fucking hell it was hot and my buttocks started sweating instantly. I fucking love the hot weather. The police tractors pulled into the road next door. I watched them. They stopped and their drivers jumped down. I thought about going over. Enrique had followed me out.

"Wha' chu think?" He asked.

"I don't know." I told him. I hadn't seen a police mobilisation like this in my life. It was the sort of thing you expect to see on TV in America. Old men were hurrying up the main road on foot, following the path of the tractors. I went over to the wall. "What's going on?" I shouted. The first few ignored me or were so out of breath they could only wheeze and so I hopped over the wall and repeated my question. "What's going on?" I asked a hurrying old man.

"Colorado Beetles!" He shouted in a shrill breathless voice.

Colorado Beetles? I'd heard of them. Them and Dung Beetles. I'd heard of Dung Beetles because they rolled up balls of poop. Stag beetle. That's another beetle I'd heard of. But Colorado Beetles? Why...

Oh yeah, I'd heard of Colorado Beetles because in about 1987 or 88 they got to Jersey and ate all the potatoes, crippling Jersey's then 97% potato-based economy. It was THE big news in Jersey from the 1980s. Nobody who grew up in Jersey can hear about Colorado Beetles without thinking of those terrible few years when we couldn't eat local potatoes. Some people turned to pasta but over a thousand people starved to death, mainly people from the older generation too set in their ways to adapt.

"That's a coincidence," I said turning to Enrique.

"What is cow... cowsin...?"

"They've found Colorado Beetles just over there. In that field. And this morning. The beetles in your office..." Enrique was staring at the police presence. "You emptied the hoover bag over there, yeah?"

"Si."

We both stared at the large crowd.

"Colorado? Where is?" Asked Enrique.

"Just over there, I said pointing to a field. That's Colorado." A policeman had produced a loud-hailer and was trying to calm the old men who were stamping about. Enrique dropped his head and went back inside. "Fucking idiot," I said out loud as I watched Enrique then after a few seconds, and one last look, I followed him. I went back to Paula.

"So, where did you get it done?" I gestured with my forehead towards her womb. "Gertrude did it," Paula replied.

"For real?" I should have guessed. "Where?"

"Her place."

"Ooof."

"Yeah."

"And? what was it like?" I asked and then, because I'm thoughtful, "do you mind talking about it?"

"It was painf-"

"I mean her house. What was it like *inside.*"

"Erm..."

I heard a coughing from behind me and turned and was loomed over by a large red-faced policemen. He was holding twelve bottles of Oasis in his strong arms. "Quick!" He said and I ran to my till and scanned them in. I scanned them all because I was panicking. I could have counted them and scanned one that many times. 12 times, as it turned out. I said he was holding 12 bottles but I didn't know that then. Everything is easy with hindsight.

"Colorado Beetles?" I said as he put the bottles in a bag. "Bad shit."

"Well," he sighed, "hopefully it's localised and we contain them but they're really belligerent little buggers. Guy from the zoo has seen nothing like it."

"Little fuckers."

"Yes."

"Perhaps they're high on heroin!" I said and laughed because I was hiding in plain sight. The policeman didn't laugh and I panicked further. "She had an abortion," I said pointing down the aisle. The policeman didn't look where I pointed, he just looked at me more. My buttocks were very sweaty indeed. "Actually these are on the house," I said, handing him back his ten pound note. The policeman took it and rushed out.

18

Kissing the Cross

I am now so fucking Catholic you would not believe it. For the last 20 years I've kept quiet about it but now that it's not cool to be a Catholic I have come out with a full-blown case of the biggest of Cs. I'm riddled with it. Last year I changed my shark's tooth for a St Christopher. The fewer practising Catholics there are the more Catholic I'm going to become.

I used to be Catholic when I was small. I was an alter boy when I was little but I, or should I say we, got fired. Me and another alter boy were messing around behind the priest. There's a bit in the service where you shake hands with people all around you. It's messed up. Anyway me and the other guy were playing to the gallery, just doing everything with a flourish, until it came time to shake hands. I crushed his hand with mine because I thought it would be funny. It wasn't funny because apparently the dumb fucker had just had an operation on his hand, didn't bother mentioning it although I guess he did have a bandage on, but he still offered me his injured hand so it was all his fault. He screamed and sobbed through the rest of the service while I sat next to him like a twat wearing a Klan outfit thinking about how much trouble I was in. I knew I was in trouble. His parents were *very* Catholic and wielded real Catholic power. My dad was just Irish. We both got fired. The point is my new found Catholicism isn't just something I've decided to do because it's now uncool and therefore cool. I've got genuine history.

I think Enrique's a Catholic. I think those people are. He has a big cross tattooed on his arm. I saw it one time he injected drugs into his arm.

On Good Friday us Catholics go to church and kiss the cross. That's the sort of batshit mad things that makes being a Catholic cool. And Midnight Mass. That's also cool. And Palm Sunday. It's a shame us Catholics don't call church 'temple'. That sounds so fucking cool, saying you're going to temple. Like Indiana Jones or a Jew. Anyway, I thought it would be good if we all went to church, it being Good Friday.

I asked Enrique if he was Catholic and he said he didn't know. I told him he probably was and he agreed. "So we'll go to church," I told him.

"Sure thing, man," he replied. 11 o'clock this morning we closed the shop and piled into my Land Rover. Enrique in the passenger seat and Marcel and Paula in the back. I felt bad making Paula sit in the back as the seats back there are narrow benches and you have to sort of perch on them. I was concerned about the state of her vagina but she'd been walking fine the last few days. As I helped her into the back I told her not to mention her abortion in church. She said she didn't even know why she was going and I told her she could stay at work then and she said she'd come with us.

It was dead anyway as most of the Islanders spend Good Friday shouting at the bears at the Zoo. I don't even know why we open. Apparently - and fuck knows where this came from - if a bear looks at you when you're talking on Good Friday then whatever you shout at it will come true. I think it's just a Jersey thing.

There's a few churches in St Ouen, near the shop, but I don't know what flavour they are. I know for sure two that are definitely Catholic. A big one in town where my dad had his funeral and the one in St Aubin. That's the one I got fired from. That's where we were going.

"Road trip!" I said as I waited for the heater plugs to heat the engine enough for it to start. This means counting to forty with the key held half-turned. When I first got the Land Rover it would start after the count of ten. After I said, "road trip!" we sat in silence for thirty-eight seconds then I turned the key fully and after the engine turning over for a bit, and in a cloud of blue smoke, the Land Rover rumbled in to life. "Road trip!" I said again and we were off.

"Why are we going to church?" Paula shouted over the drone of the engine as we headed past The Amaizin' Maze.

"We're going to kiss the cross." I shouted back. Enrique looked at me from the passenger seat. "Kiss the cross," I told him. He shifted in the seat and looked over his shoulder at Paula, his expression not changing. "Jesus!" I said ,"you kiss Jesus on the cross," I told him. "Not the actual cross."

"Jesus?" Enrique shouted. The Land Rover was really noisy.

"You call him he-zuss! Jesus! A model of him! Not the real..." We drove past the Co-op in St Peter, down Beaumont Hill and along the front to St

Aubin. We parked opposite the garage and piled out of the Land Rover. It was sunny and warm out of the wind.

"So *what* are we going to do?" Asked Paula. We were all smoking.

> "We're going to go over there and kiss the cross."

> "Kiss the cross?"

"Not the cross. Jesus, you kiss Jesus. A model of him." Paula was doing that thing that woman do in car parks - getting right in the way. She was stopping traffic from easily driving around the car park by being a foot or two too far out from the cars and I pulled her over so we were stood in a tighter group at the back of the Land Rover.

> "Why?" She asked.

> "Oh my Christ," I exhaled. "The fuck should I know?"

> "What?" asked Enrique.

"I thought you'd know, with your tattoo," I gestured

to his forearm that was covered with his white shirt sleeve and white suit sleeve. He looked at his covered forearm and then pulled his sleeves up revealing a large cross.

"Dis?" Asked Enrique, "Dis aeroplane."

"That's not a fucking aeroplane. It's a cross," I told him. I was getting cross.

Enrique studied his tattoo. "Pilot sit there," he said pointing at the end of the long bit. "Why's it so square? Where's the tail?" I asked him. "Where are the windows? It's a cross. Come on, cross," I told the group after I'd checked for oncoming traffic. Although they were all adults I was sure if I took my eyes off them for a minute they would run out into the road and be killed.

We crossed to the church and went in. It was dark and cool inside. There were small recesses in the granite wall next to the door that were filled with holy water. You were supposed to do something with it but I couldn't remember what so I just dipped my hand in and then rubbed my hands together like I do when I visit a hospital. The others all copied me.

The church was pretty empty because we were

early so we got seats right at the front. In the next five minutes the church filled. "Good timing, eh?" I told the others. They nodded. Marcel was studying the hymn book that he'd found in the wooden shelf thing that was in front of us.

Paula huffed and puffed a bit to show she wasn't happy to be there. Before the priest came out she whispered, "can't we go to the zoo?" I just looked at her like she was mental then the priest did come out and he started talking. At various points people stood, sat down, knelt and stood up. I took my cues from other people and Enrique, Paula and Marcel took their cues from me. There was singing but none of us sang. I found out what song was being sung in the song book and pointed to the words. The others crowded around me and nodded. I stole a few glances around and nobody was looking at us for not singing. The service went on a bit but it was probably better than being at work.

"It's better than being at work," I whispered to Paula.

"Not really," she replied.

Then it was time to kiss the cross. I saw part of myself in the two alter boys who carried the cross to the middle of the stage bit of a church, at the end of the aisle. I didn't remember doing it myself when I was an altar boy but maybe I had. The cross was about five foot tall with a Jesus nailed to it. As we were at the front we went first. It was like getting off a plane.

> Enrique was closest to the aisle and so he went out first. Then Paula and then me and then behind me, Marcel. "Just kiss it," I told Enrique. Enrique looked unsure and then he looked at the priest who nodded at him and then Enrique bent down and kissed Jesus. The alter boys giggled and one of them wiped Jesus' mouth with a cloth or wet wipe or something. Paula kissed Jesus next. I was watching the alter boys, they were on the verge of losing it. I smiled. I'd been there. It was my turn. I was confident, I kissed Jesus and heard the alter boys stifle laughter. That annoyed me a bit actually, I'd kissed Jesus with supreme confidence. I didn't see Marcel kiss Jesus as after kissing him you walked to the other end of your wooden bench thing and shuffled along until you were back where you started. There you sat down, job done.

I watched the other church goers kiss the cross. At first I didn't notice anything different about how they were doing it but then in a terrible instant I realised every single other person was kissing Jesus' feet. We'd all kissed him on the mouth.

I knew you kissed his feet. I knew that but I was just doing what the others did without thinking. I looked up at the priest, he was glaring at me. I looked at Paula and saw that somewhere in her mind she had realised we had done it different than anybody else. She started pointing at the crucifix and then turned to me. Before she could speak I said, "I know." I looked at the alter boys, they kept glancing over, and then turning right away and I watched their shoulders shake. A few people who filed past us after they had kissed Jesus' feet looked at me and shook their head.

The cross was eventually taken away and although initially it had been cool in the church it now felt hot, too hot, my face was burning.

The priest droned on for a what seemed like hours. More standing, kneeling, not singing. We did the bit where you shook hands but I didn't meet eyes with anybody whose hand I took from the row behind and just when I thought it would never end it did. The priest said something, the people in the crowd said something and then people were leaving. It took us ages to get out as most of the people in the church were old and only there to socialize and because we were at the front we were furthest from the door.

Outside the air had never felt fresher, the breeze that had been warm an hour earlier felt chilly and wonderful. I wafted my Spar polo shirt a few times to cool my torso.

"Fucking hell," I said to Paula when we'd reached an acceptable distance from old church goers. "I'm not bringing you idiots again."

"Let's go to the zoo!" She said.

"What, to shout at a bear?" I snorted.

"Can't be any worse dan dat, man," said Enrique.

"Yeah, that was fucked," said Marcel. The first words he'd said since leaving. I nodded, they were right in a way, it was fucked but I wasn't going to the zoo. It was five miles away and cost about £20 each to get in. Fuck that. No *fucking* way, my friend.

50 minutes later we were in the queue to enter the Zoo. You could see it was packed inside from the turnstile as we drove past. It had taken us 20 minutes to walk from the overflow car park. The noise coming from inside was tremendous. It was £20 each to get in. I was amazed that inside we could actually see a bear as the bear enclosure has a very tall tree trunk or man made pole in the centre of it. The bear was sitting on top of it chewing something. Thousands of people were trying to get its attention.

Bear! Bear! Cure this! Need new windows! Bring this kid back to life! I need ten grand! Leukaemia! Bear! BEAR! *BEAR!*

> The bear was playing it cool, looking at its feet and sometimes the sky. I turned to the others and raised my eyebrows. Paula nodded and then I heard her shout, "Bear!" She shouted. "Look after my baby!" I looked to the bear who didn't look to Paula. I then looked at Paula.

> "*What?*" I shouted, but Paula was shouting for the bear. "Bear! Tell my baby I love her!"

I looked at Enrique and shook my head, his eyes flicked to me and back to the bear. He was licking his lips nervously. Before I could impart on him just exactly how fucked Paula was being by using nothing but my expressive facial expression Enrique shouted something in foreign. I looked at him with my questioning face and Enrique mimed steering a car. I nodded and looked back at the bear. People I didn't know were shouting right next to my ear. No shame at all. I turned the other way and saw Marcel. He was shouting something at the bear. He was shouting in French and sweating in French. His face as red as the red bit of the Tricolor.

> I'd had enough, "Bear!" I shouted in a funny voice to show I was only fucking around, "Bear! I want to..." *What should I shout?* "I want to be happy!" The bear didn't look at me. I chuckled then licked

my lips. "Bear!" I shouted but it didn't turn. "Bear!! Help me, bear!" I shouted.

At 4pm we were ushered away. We'd been shouting at the bear for over two hours with no success. At one point it had sort of almost glanced in my direction while chewing lazily on what looked like bark. I heard Paula shout frantically beside me but I pushed her to the ground and waved at the bear while screaming at the top of my voice but the bear was already looking at its feet again.

In the gift shop Enrique bought us all a new Cookie Maxibon which we don't stock yet. We ate them on the way to the Land Rover. They're gorgeous. Was I happy eating it? For sure. *Perhaps there was something in the whole bear thing*, I thought, smiling through tearful eyes. And then I drove us back to the shop in total fucking silence.

19

Egg

We were all pretty sheepish in the shop this morning. Don't really know what happened with the bear yesterday but I definitely shouted out stuff I didn't want anybody but the bear to hear. Hopefully nobody noticed and we're all in the same boat so it's not too bad. It's not like when I ruin work Christmas parties and then have to show up on the Monday. It's like more like when we *all* ruin the Christmas party.

I didn't see Enrique at all until mid-morning when he stuck his head out of the office and beckoned me ominously. We're not doing hot food today. Today's a weird day. It's like the eye of the storm - the walls of the storm being Good Friday and Easter Sunday and even those days are more like the calm before the storm. And Monday's a Bank Holiday so today is a write off really. It's nothing like a storm but it was busy. Paula was behind the counter with me so I could go into Enrique's office, no sweat.

"What?" I asked him looking around for unlikely animal invaders. A koala bear or something. A giraffe. There were none but on his desk was a twelve pack of eggs. A dozen, in Olde English. He'd cracked them all into an empty ice cream tub. There were also Easter eggs - unwrapped and smashed - and a raw chicken. *Here we go*, I thought to myself.

Enrique waved for me to sit down and then he sat down in his chair. "What?" I asked him again. I watched as Enrique made a clicking noise with his mouth and tried to formulate what he wanted to say. He puckered his mouth and moved his puckered mouth across his face and then back again. "What?" I asked.

Enrique looked up at me and then down to the produce that lay between us like a fox's smorgasbord. He moved his hands over the produce like a chess player with his back against the wall in the World Chess Championship Final. I thought he was going to pick up some chocolate but then, with a sigh, he picked up the raw chicken. It was unwrapped but still on the polystyrene tray He held it up deftly with one hand and even managed to spin. He looks like a waiter. He should be a waiter.

"Dis?" He said.

"A chicken," I replied although I didn't really think that's what he wanted to know.

"Where dis from?"

"Vietnam," I told him. I actually knew that even with the packaging gone because I'd noticed it ages ago. On that day I'd been so bored I read the chicken wrapper. I was disappointed though not surprised. Food miles are a fact of life.

"Non," said Enrique. He was being pretty serious. He put the chicken down and I wondered how long it had been out of the fridge. "How does a chicken g'happen?"

"That's the age old question!" I told him wishing, as I do, that my life was being filmed and people could hear me say these smart things.

"De a jold question?"

"Age old."

"A jold?"

"Age. Old. Old. It's the old question."

"How does chicken happen?"

"Yeah, you know? What came first, the chicken or the egg? Nobody knows for sure. It's a... thing."

"I know," said Enrique nodding and looking at the big mess in front of us.

"Oh yeah?"

"Not de fucking egg, man."

"Okay," I agreed, I didn't care.

"Look!" He pointed into the tub that was empty of ice cream but about a 7th full of egg yolks and the stuff in the egg that isn't the yolk. Something like album, it's called, I think. Alblumen. Nah, don't know.

"Eggs," I said.

"No chicken."

"No, eggs."

"Eggs yes, chicken no."

"No," I agreed.

"Where is chicken?"

"You mean why isn't there a chicken in the egg?"

"Yes why no chicken? It is a mystery, no?"

"Well, Enrique," I said, this time it was me who took a few seconds to formulate what I wanted to say. I scratched my lip. Had a spot there the other day. "See, a chicken lays eggs anyway. Everyday. They only turn into an *actual* chicken if they're fertilised." I hoped that was the end of the matter.

"Okay, fertilltillasized with a... a... a dick?"

"Yeah?"

"Like Paula was fertilltillasized by a dick."

"Bit harsh," I said and then laughed at my own great joke. *Where were those cameras?* "But yeah. Fertilised." Was that the word? It sounded weird now I was hearing it so much. Like when I said 'lorry' so many times in quick succession it was no longer a word in the English language. Inseminated. That was what I meant. *Was it?*

"She no lay hegg,"

"No." I agreed. Paula did not lay an egg.

"So..." said Enrique again looking over his army battalions spread out on the desk. He picked up the chicken again. "Where is the dick?"

I tried to resist. I really did but I couldn't and I pointed at him and said, "there!" I imagined gales of laughter from people watching that on TV. Enrique didn't get it. "That's probably a girl chicken," I told him.

He lifted it off the tray. "Dis de fanny?" He asked me pointing to one end of the chicken. "I don't know," I told him honestly.

"Or dis?" He asked pointing at the other end.

"I really don't know." I couldn't actually work out which end of the chicken was which or which way up it would have went when it was alive. Enrique mulled this over. "Okay?" I said going through the standing up preliminaries which means smacking my thighs. This shows I'm about to stand up.

"Bah, bah, bah!" Barked Enrique with his left palm raised to stop me standing.

"So. A man chicken has a dick?"

"Yes," I sighed, but now I wasn't sure. I'd never seen a chicken's dick. I certainly wasn't going to tell Enrique a man chicken is called a cock, that would have been like that time that whole Spanish family tried to teach me the word manana meant 'tomorrow', but it also meant 'morning.' They were shouting over each other like idiots for a hour.

Enrique opened his top drawer and then his middle draw. What he wanted was in his middle drawer. It was a pad of paper. He took it out. I watched. Enrique then blew my mind by drawing a brilliant chicken.

"That's awesome!" I told him, genuinely *very* impressed. I didn't know he could draw. It wasn't like he'd copied the chicken he had, this was a real chicken.

"Dis woman chicken," he said tapping the chicken with his pen.

"Okay."

He then drew another great chicken right behind the first chicken, when Enrique draws he sticks his tongue out of the corner of his mouth. "Dis man chicken," he said. "Yup," I agreed.

"Now, problem," He said moving his pen over his drawing but not drawing. "How big?" He asked pointing to the undercarriage of the man chicken and the back of the woman chicken. "How big dat?" He asked.

"About eight inches," I answered with a chuckle. Mother-fucker was right. How the *hell* do chickens happen?

"S'impossible. No chicken has eight inch dick, man. No way."

"No, you're right," I agreed my voice high with agreement and surprise. We both looked at his drawing. I tilted my head to the side, as far as it would go. "Maybe if you turn the woman chicken upside down?" I offered but it was a weak suggestion. Enrique opened his drawers again.

"No zig-zags!"

"What?"

"No zig-zags,"

"Zig-zags?"

Enrique did closing and opening Vs with his fingers. "Zig-zags." "Scissors."

"Oh scissors. If we have scissors I could..."

Paula knocked and opened the door. I turned. Enrique didn't have to. He was facing her. "What are you doing?" She asked. She was annoyed. We'd been ages.

"Hey, how do chickens fuck?" I asked her. She removed her head and closed the door. We went back to Enrique's drawing. "Maybe they back into each other?" I said drawing my hands together.

"No," said Enrique. "No possible. Need a back dick for dat."

We sat there for another few minutes looking at the picture until I broke the silence. "I better get back out there," I said to my boss. He was staring at his picture and nodding. He tilted his head. "I better get back out there," I said again. I clapped my hands onto my thighs and then got back out there.

20

Trading Standards

You know, hindsight is 50/50 but I actually noticed something was up for sure. I just didn't say anything. Last couple of days strange people have been buying sausage rolls. Normally somebody who buys a sausage roll is a man, aged 18-55 and wearing soiled work clothing, but twice this week a lady wearing a skirt has bought them. No self respecting lady would eat a sausage roll so given those events it wasn't *massive* surprise when a middle-aged man wearing make-up to make him look like an old man came in. He was heading to the hot food counter and to Paula but I stopped him with a rumbustious greeting.

> "Hello," I said studying his face which was clearly wrong and fake.

> "Erm, hi. Do you sell sausage rolls?" He asked. "*Full* size sausage rolls?"

> "Who wants to know?" I asked returning the question with the ease of a Eastern European tennis player returning the noodle-armed serve of one of our lot.

> Then the man pulled off his face and said, "Bill Zeon, Channel TV's Baddy Busters."

I'd never watched it, didn't recognize his real face. His fake face looked more like a face I knew. His fake face was a bit like Johnny Socks' face. But I was cool, like I said, I had been expecting the exact thing to happen so I was completely relaxed.

> "So then, sausage rolls," said Bill, he was out of breath for some reason. A camera crew momentarily got jammed *in* then came bustling *through* the doors.

> I nodded at them then I turned back to Bill. This was it, they were filming my life. All my dreams come true. "Yeah, we sell sausage rolls," I told him.

"What of it?"

"Well we've had numerous complaints about the size of your sausage rolls."

"We cut the ends off them and eat the ends," I told him flatly, standing my ground. Bill Zeon didn't expect such honesty.

"Isn't that ripping off your customers?" Bill turned to the camera for a moment. "Sure is, fuck 'em." I told him. I turned to the camera and nodded.

"Well I'm sure your customers will be pleased to hear the... the..."

"Contempt?"

"The contempt with which you view them."

"I don't think they will be pleased. Why do you think they'll be pleased?"

"The point is you *are* ripping them off."

"Mah," I said which isn't even a word, it was just a sound. I looked back to the camera. Bill was really

143

struggling for what to say next. He'd expected me to run away crying.

"Have you got anything you'd like to say to your customers who, by your own admission, you're ripping off."

"Erm," I said. I looked at my hands and extended the thumb and forefinger on each. One of them would make an L shape when viewed from not where I was. "Which one's an L?" I asked Bill Zeon. He looked at both of my hands before pointing to the right one. I then stuck that one against my forehead and turned to the camera.

"That's it, is it?"

"I could sing?"

"You could sing?"

"Nah, not really, I'm a horrible singer."

It was Bill's turn to talk to the camera. "Well, there we have it, Spar St Ouen, quite happy to be rippin -"

"Can't you think of a term other than ripping off?"

I asked loudly. "You've said it, like, four or five times." Bill sighed at this then looked at the woman who had come in with the camera men. "What do you reckon?" He asked her. She told him to give it a couple more minutes. Bill stood for a few seconds looking at his feet. Then he looked up. "So?" He asked. "How do you..." he trailed off then muttered, "that's no good."

"How would I feel if my mother bought undersized sausage rolls?" I said, helping him out. "Okay," said Bill. "How would you feel?"

"What?"

"If your mother came in here and was sold undersized sausage rolls?"

"How would I feel?"

"Yes?"

"Like dog shit."

"So why do it to other people then?" Bill liked that, his voice was strained and the sentence rose at the end.

"I guess I'm just a dick, Bill."

"Well," said Bill doing a fake TV laugh, "I can't argue with that."

"With what?"

"What you just said."

"What did I just say?"

"About you being a..." He couldn't say *dick* because he was on TV. "An unpleasant character."

"I didn't say that." I told him.

"Well I think we're done here," said Bill to the camera. He looked at the lady who shrugged and nodded. Bill looked back at me and said, "thanks," with some sarcasm and, "I guess we'll be seeing you on the Baddy's Corner." I didn't know what that was.

"Will you or won't you?"

"We will."

"Where you going now," I asked.

"We're leaving," he replied.

"I don't think so," I said rushing behind them and blocking the door. "What's your hurry?" I held my arms out but was careful not to touch any of them as I didn't want to get charged with assault.

"Can we leave please?" Asked the lady.

"If you can somehow walk through me, then yes."

The three people holding equipment, the lady and Bill all looked at each other. One of the men holding equipment was quite big, he stepped forward. I screamed like a girl and he froze. They all looked at each other again.

"COWABUNGA!" Shouted Enrique appearing from stage left (right actually. My right.) The shovel he was swinging had already gone through over 180 degrees before Bill even saw Enrique. Whether he had enough time to register what was happening before the shovel struck the back of his head is for the coroner to decide. Enrique leapt back on his toes and spun the shovel like a Chinaman. The other four were huddled together and edging my way, towards the door I was blocking. I lifted my leg and gave the huddle a shove back with my foot.

"Don't!" Cried the woman at Enrique who was stood poised to strike. Enrique growled, a feral smile on his face. He made a dummy move forward. The woman whimpered.

"Listen..." said one of the men with his palm raised in supplication. I didn't want to hear what he had to say. I flicked my eyes to Enrique who read my instructions and in a flash he hit that guy with the shovel and then the shovel was a propeller in Enrique's dexterous hands. It was spinning so fast it did that thing when it looks like it's going backwards. Enrique edged towards the last three standing.

"Better watch out!" I told them but they could do nothing. I turned away as the shovel hit. I heard a wet chopping sound and was splattered with the blood and chunks. I didn't mind, my polo shirt had been dirty when I put it on. Only a small coffee stain. I was going to take it straight back off but then I thought, *well, if I'd put it on THEN spilled a small amount of coffee on it I wouldn't be ashamed and take it off in a massive hurry so I may as well just wear it.* But I was conflicted. It was different putting on a slightly stained T-shirt rather than putting a clean one on and then slightly staining it. I didn't know why it was different, but it was different.

I looked down at the pile of meat, "I told you to watch out," I said to it and laughed. Enrique laughed and Paula laughed. When we stopped laughing I told Enrique that I would go and set fire to their van which was in the car park. Enrique said he would put the bodies in the field where he'd put the beetles and the Squirrel and Paula said she'd clean up because she was a woman. I forgot to include Marcel. I always do because he's usually outside.

That's what I was daydreaming when the woman came in looking for marjoram. It was an angry daydream because my wife had annoyed me when I was eating my breakfast. She'd been talking about a person I didn't know who was a pilot. It was big news. Some guy I possibly walk past when taking the kids to school is a pilot. I'd been eating my eggs when she told me about the pilot. "Why are you telling me this?" I'd asked. She just thought it was interesting. *Yeah right!* No she didn't, she was telling me to make me feel bad about myself. Because I'm not a pilot or a lawyer or somebody who goes away on business trips. It worked.

She was very polite, the woman looking for marjoram. The woman didn't look thick, in fact quite the opposite, she looked like she could have worked at the Large Hadron Collider. She wasn't looking for sausage rolls, that much was obvious. She looked scholarly and perhaps worked in a college.

"Do you have marjoram?" She asked.

"Margarine?" I said to the woman.

"Oh no, marjoram, it's like... erm, oregano."

"Orangina?"

The woman laughed. "It's a herb, dried. The little pots." She showed me what little was with her fingers.

"No, I don't know what they are, What's a herb?" I asked, staring at her impassively. I know what oregano is, and herbs, and yes, the little pots, I even know of those. I was simply challenging this woman's perception and at the time it seemed like the right thing to do but actually writing it out now it doesn't seem quite so funny. We don't sell herbs anyway. The woman laughed nervously and looked around the shop.

"The.. the... pots," she said. She was still demonstrating the size of the pots with her thumb and forefinger while looking around the shop but not really looking. I was pleased she had begun to stutter.

"Pots?" I said. The woman turned
to me and smiled.

"Okay thanks," she said and headed
for the exit.

"Thanks, what is that? I don't even know?" I said
and held a finger to my chin and she hesitated
momentarily but then continued out of the door
and across to her car with her head down. I laughed
when she dropped her keys.

21

April Fool

I entered the shop still muttering like Yosemite Sam and the fact that the big lights weren't on didn't bother me. I went straight to Enrique's office to hang my coat up. I opened the door and was met with the sight of Enrique - his face horribly deformed - staring at himself in the mirror. I didn't expect that and my anger turned to fear. Instantly. I think my heart actually stopped for a while. It's safe to say I nearly shit. Enrique turned to me, but even then it was two or three seconds before my brain actually processed that he was wearing a mask. It was a wretched mask, possibly supposedly an approximation of a US politician or perhaps an actor. It was a poor quality mask.

"What are you doing?" I asked, still full of fear. Enrique didn't answer, his eyes - the only part of his face that were real and shiny - flicked over to his desk and then back to me. I looked at his desk. Laid out on the desk was a pair of handcuffs, some rope, one of those ping-pong ball mouth strap things and a pile of material, clothing or blankets I do not know. Enrique's hat was also on the desk. "Okay," I announced to Enrique who was still still and still facing his face at me and then I hung my coat up and left his office. I put the lights on and felt a little bit safer because nothing bad happens when it's light.

A few minutes later Enrique emerged without his mask and wearing his hat. *Was he a hacker?* I'd asked myself in the time it took him to emerge. I watched him. He was pretending to look for something down the aisles. He was clearly pretending to look preoccupied but he wasn't, he was approaching me covertly. When he was a few paces from me and staring down one of the aisles pointing at nothing in particular and pretending to count he suddenly wheeled on his heels, pointed at me and shouted, "April fool!"

"What was?" I asked him. Enrique had a wide grin plastered to his face. He cocked a thumb back to his office. His pose was almost Michael Angelo's David in appearance. "*That* was an April Fool?"

"I got chu!" He said still grinning and leaning forward with his thumb still cocked back.

"It's, like, the twentieth," I said. Enrique laughed stood upright and then went over to the window. The car park was empty apart from his Cadillac in the disabled bay. "Of May."

"It'll be a nice day," he said nodding and gazing out with his hands held behind his back. I couldn't help looking at his hands and wondering what despicable acts he had in store for them.

"Enrique?" I asked without thinking too hard. He turned and lifted his eyebrows. "What was that in there?"

"Dat in der?"

"Yeah, that in there, what *was* that in there?"

"Dat was notink." Enrique held my gaze and I

backed down. Lowered my gaze. When I looked back he was again staring out of the window. "Come on people!" He shouted and then clapped and rubbed his murderous rapey hands together.

"You're happy today then?"

"Si Si. Chu ever got a royalty cheque?" He asked.

"A royalty cheque?"

"Chu ever get one?"

"No."

"I get one today."

"What for?" I asked. The only thing I could think of was perhaps he had recorded some shit folk shit back in Colombia and it was on the radio.

"Wha' fo'?" He asked me back. I didn't respond. "For being *awesome*." He stretched the word awesome for a while until it faded to nothing like a Scotsman in the sun.

"They don't give you royalty cheques

just for being awesome."

"Chu see, man, it's from Spa," he told me and I supposed that this was nothing more than the second in Enrique's fucked up, nonsensical series of April Fool tricks and so I read the paper.

It was supposed to rain all day but actually it was quite nice, the showers held off and out of the wind it was pretty warm so we had ice-creams outside, around the back.

Mid-afternoon I saw Stan's car pull up. Can't remember what car I said Stan drove last time but this time it was different. It was a Mitsubishi Evo (Evolution) VII (Seven). Enrique was reading the inside of the dire selection on birthday cards we stock and chuckling to himself. "It's Stan!" I shouted. Enrique replaced the card and rubbed his hands together.

"Moony time!" He said. He then lifted his fists and really clenched them so his whole body vibrated. It was funny as fuck.

"Wassup!" Said Stan when he entered. Enrique was now beside me.

"Wassup!" I replied.

"Stan," said Enrique politely. I should have said just said hello. Stan put his folder on the counter.

"You got my email then?" He asked Enrique. Enrique nodded. He was breathing hard. Nearly panting. I stepped away from him as I hate people breathing near me. "You know why I'm here?" He asked me.

"Not really," I told him honestly.

"Well, let me just say," said Stan suddenly serious, "that I am here in the capacity as a *mate*, yeah?" We nodded. "Forget I'm the big boss, yeah?" We nodded. Stan isn't the big *big* boss. He's Enrique's boss but he's not the *boss* boss. I don't know who is. It's not Stan. He's definitely not a mate either. Truth be told he's a bit of a dick. "Cool beans," said Stan. I didn't know what that meant. Stan opened his folder and took out a sheet of paper and placed it on the counter. Enrique grabbed it scanned it front and back and then put it down. It wasn't a cheque. Looked more like an order form. It was an order form. Stan picked it up and gave it to Enrique. "What is that?"

"Dis? Dis order form," said Enrique proudly.

"For?"

Enrique read it. "Three hundred Maxibon Cookie cream ices." I'd been asking Enrique to do it ever since we had one at the zoo. I didn't think he'd done it though, fair play to him.

"Ice creams?" Asked Stan. "Three hundred?" Enrique studied the form, nodded and put it down. "You see these tills?" Said Stan pointing at the tills. *Yeah Stan, we could see the tills that are right there you fucking dummy, we're not blind.* "These are all computerised, yeah?" We nodded. The computers are computerised. Makes sense. "So that *we* know what you sell, yeah?"

"H'okay," said Enrique but he didn't understand where this was going.

"Last summer you sold twelve Twisters and three Cornettos."

"H'okay," said Enrique who was now slightly grinning. He didn't get it at all. "That's fifteen ice creams. That's it. Fifteen."

"H'okay," said Enrique, he was clearly trying to keep track of all these massive numbers in his head.

"Fifteen ice creams. Last summer you had over twelve hundred ice creams delivered." "H'okay," said Enrique now looking puzzled.

I had to interject. "The freezer broke."

"Sure," said Stan.

"And those kids, remember Enrique? The little thieves?" I shook my head to convey how bad the thieving children had been. "Buggers." Stan might have been a dick but he wasn't so incredibly stupid though.

"Listen guys, I used to work on the floor. I know how it is. You've got to make this job bearable, yeah?" I didn't nod or do anything. It was likely a trap. "There are perks, right?" I didn't respond. "You probably have 'Ice Cream Time."

"Ice cream time!" Shouted Paula from the back of the shop.

Stan nodded his head towards her voice. Enrique

was still looking puzzled. "But you can't take the piss," Stan continued. He looked at Enrique and then me. "These Maxibon Cookie things, these are *new*. It's a premium product. People are going... *I'm* going to notice three hundred of those going AWOL, understand?" I nodded ever so slightly. "Eat the Mini-Milks. Or Calippos." I nodded again but it was a fake nod. Calippos are a waste of time, I'd rather go without. "So you're not getting the Maxibon Cookie," he said and then put the order form back in his folder. I nodded. Enrique was still looking puzzled but nodded too. "Okay then guys?" Said Stan looking around the empty shop. "Okay." I said. Stan put his thumb up and then started for his car. I thought about asking him for a Slush Puppie machine but Enrique ruined it. "My cheque?" Said Enrique, rather timidly. "Cheque?" Squinted Stan.

"My... royalty cheque?"

"*What?*"

"De email? A... a cheque?"

Stan thought about this for a seconds. "A reality check?"

"Si!" Said Enrique, the smile returning to his face.

Stan looked at me and then to Enrique. "That was it."

"Oh, h'okay!" Said Enrique and he looked at the counter but didn't move.

Stan looked at me again and then said, "ciao," and left.

Enrique was lifting things off the counter and looking down the back of the counter. He spent half an hour looking for it. He's a bell-end. Later in the night, when I was home, I watched him furtively lead a nervous looking young woman into my garage/ his house.

I couldn't really see if she was frightened, it was too dark, but it's a fair assumption - Enrique leads you *anywhere* at gone midnight and that's got to give you butterflies in your tummy. I could see that Enrique was carrying a rucksack and that was unusual for him. I guessed it was filled with the mask and the other ghastly accoutrements of torture he had been fucking about with in the shop. Although I was sure that I couldn't be seen in the darkness of my kitchen I stood stock still and watched them go in.

I reckon Enrique has killed a person before, his reaction when I jokingly said he had at those awards that time pretty much confirmed it but then he's from Colombia. I doubt there are many Colombians who haven't killed at least one other Colombian. I don't even care. Rape is a different story. It'd be bad enough if he was driving around doing it but doing it in my garage where my treadmill lives is taking the biscuit.

Listen, I'm talking about rape, like it's no big deal. I'm blasé and flippant. I'll spoil this for you. I'd made a *massive* mistake with my assumption that made an ass out of me.

Enrique *wasn't* being monstrous. I wouldn't be telling anybody about something like that - I'd be giving police statements. But that's with the benefit of hindsight, something I have and you don't. At the time I genuinely thought he was planning to rape that poor woman and so I after looking in the fridge and eating a sausage - nothing makes me happier than when there are cooked sausages in the fridge - I went out to put a stop to it.

I'm not frightened of Enrique. He's my boss but I'm his landlord, he's not going to fuck with me or he'll be living in his car and so out I went. It was *freezing* so I went back in the house and got my coat. I went back out and had a cigarette to steady my nerves. I don't normally smoke on my own property but my wife was asleep and this was a special situation.

I went to the side door on the garage and couldn't really hear anything and so I knocked. I heard something fall over inside the garage but nobody opened it. I knocked again and counted to twenty before trying the handle. The handle was obviously being held from the other side by a human as it softly gave a smidge. "Enrique!" I shouted quietly.

I tried to force the handle down to open the door but Enrique must've been giving it everything on the other-side and the handle felt like it would break before I could out-muscle him. The door handles were £3 from B&Q. *No point putting good ones on for Enrique* I'd thought when buying them. My thriftiness had come home to roost so I let go of the handle and knocked again and again quietly shouted his name. I again counted to twenty with no plan for what I was going to do when I got there.

I didn't get there as when I got to twelve the door opened. Enrique was there. He wasn't wearing his hat. Normally when Enrique isn't wearing his hat his hair is impeccably swept back but now it was a right old mess. He'd been wearing his mask.

> "What are you doing?" I asked, giving him an opportunity to confess and repent.

> "Nothink," he replied. He was holding the door open about a quarter. Not enough for me to see everything. I could the garage was lit only by candles.

> "Can I come in?" I asked.

"No," he replied, his mouth moving about under his nose. I wasn't expecting him to say no. "No?"

"No."

"It's my garage!" I told him.

"S'my house. Chu cannot come in when chu wan."

"You're a lawyer now are you?"

"I see chu tomorrow," said Enrique, going to close the door. I was incredulous. I stood watching as he closed the door, his head bowed. Just before it closed completely I pushed it hard.

"Hold on a minute," I said forcing the door open and barging in. I looked around for the woman but I couldn't see her and Enrique's garage house doesn't have anywhere you could conceal a woman. It was pretty dark. The candles were arranged on a table as if on an alter. I saw the one place where the woman could be concealed. His large luggage chest with Colombian stickers on it and then I understood and felt like an idiot. I breathed a massive sigh of relief. "Is she in there?" I asked him while walking over to it. Enrique nodded again looking to the floor. I knocked on the chest and shouted, "hello!"

"Help!" cried a voice from inside. I laughed.

"Fucks sake, Enrique!" I exclaimed. "How long have you been doing this?"

"Bout ten... fourteen years."

"Ten or fourteen years!" I marvelled. "Why didn't you say anything?"

Enrique shook his head a muttered something that could have been the word 'shame.' I took it as him saying the word shame.

"Nothing to be ashamed of!" I told him chuckling. "I think it's brilliant. You've been a magician all this time and not said anything." I heard the woman shout help again. I knocked on the chest and said, "don't worry, he'll have you out in a minute!"

I looked at Enrique, he was eyeing me suspiciously. "I mean it, Enrique, I fucking love this shit. You got any balloons?"

"Balloons?" He asked. "No."

"Shame, I can do balloon animals. That's not really magic though... go on, do a trick!" I urged. "No." He said.

"Okay," I told him. "But when you're happy with it you have to put on show for us. For the shop. Have you got a stage name?"

"Yeah," said Enrique following me to the door but not saying what his stage name was. "I'm not even going to tell you what I thought you were doing," I told him and took one last look around, shook my head and returned to my kitchen. I nearly choked on a sausage while chuckling when I heard a shriek from the garage. And then it was silent.

22

Apples

Been eating a load of apples this week. Thing is they all have these little stickers on them. They're there so shop assistants don't charge for Braeburns when they're actually Royal Galas. Insider tip, wanna save money? Change the stickers over on the apples. It's worth it. Problem I've had at home is when I take an apple from the fruit bowl I take the sticker off and put it on a different apple. Of course eventually you end up with a couple of apples covered in fucking stickers. A real ball-ache.

23

Blackmail

"You in?" Asked Paula and I was on the spot. I can normally worm my way out of most things with my super sharp brain, but this?

"You're not getting it now, are you?" I asked. I needed time to think.

"Soon," she said ominously.

"Okay," I said folding my bottom lip into a point and thinking hard. I didn't mean, 'okay I'm in'. I meant, 'okay, it's good I have time to think'.

Paula was talking about buying a ticket for the Jersey Hospice Lottery. We don't have the National Lottery over here and instead every year the Hospice - which I think is a hospital for horses - run a lottery. The good thing is the first prize is one million pounds. Not too shabby. The bad thing is the tickets are one hundred pounds each. But the good thing is there's a limited number of tickets. But they're one hundred pounds each, that's bad. It's a bit fucking stupid really as you'd need to have won the thing to buy a ticket and because of the huge investment required syndicates form to buy a ticket. Work syndicates. One had formed at work like a moss mask on the face of a corpse buried in a damp meadow. Enrique was in, Marcel was in and Paula was in. Paula asked if I wanted in. I said... I've done that.

Clearly I didn't want in. In an ideal scenario nobody I knew would have a chance of winning it and then I wouldn't have to worry about trying to win it, you know, to be better than them. I didn't want to give Paula £25 and I didn't much want to give the Hospice £25. So I thought about what would happen if I wasn't in. It only took a second, in fact I didn't even need to think about it. They'd win it for sure. It was obvious. If I wasn't in then they'd win. Each of them would win £333,333 and I'd be the World's biggest dickhead and there'd be articles about me in the media

However if I *did* give them £25 then obviously we wouldn't win and I'd be £25 out of pocket. I should just give them the £25 because that's literally what I would be doing, I'd be giving Paula and Enrique and Marcel £25 because we wouldn't win. There isn't another option. Or is there? *There must be,* I assured myself.

Enrique came out of his office. He looked smug, like he was going to win £333,333 and I wasn't. The arsehole. He was eating coleslaw and pitta bread. He was using the pitta for a scoop, leaning forward slightly.

"Okay?" I asked. He nodded. He couldn't talk as he had a mouth full of coleslaw. Then he turned and went back into his office, still leaning forward slightly. He banged the door open with his shoulder. My head hurt. £25 is quite a lot of money to just give away. It wouldn't break the bank but I really didn't want to do it. I cursed the idiots at work for making my life so very complicated. Why couldn't nothing ever happen? Why must people do things? What the hell would Enrique do with that kind of money? Or Paula? Fucking hell. I could talk them out of buying a ticket? Would that work? That *could* work and we'd maintain the status quo. It was worth a shot.

"Paula," I said walking towards Paula. I hadn't prepared what I was going to say but I felt confident it would come to me on the hoof.

"Are you in?" She asked.

"You know..." I began.

"Decide *now*, right now," she said. She didn't look interested and that was the unsettling part. "Don't be an idiot," I told her. "I just..."

"That's it, you're not in." She blew a bubble. This one didn't pop, it deflated. I watched it. "What?" I said, snapping out of it. Ooh, *this wasn't right at all*. "Don't be a cunt," I said. I didn't mean to say that. I was a caged tiger. "You stupid cunt," I added making things worse. Paula was looking at me. It didn't seem like I'd outwitted her, quite to opposite in fact. "I..."

"Too late," she said "We didn't want you in it anyway."

"I wasn't fucking *going* to be in it anyway, fuckface," I kind of lied, it had still all been up in the air.

"Cool," said Paula.

"I know it is," I told her and then I headed back

to the counter wearing a pained expression but keeping my ears relaxed so she couldn't tell. *What the fuck was happening to me?* I should have just stolen £25 from the till there and then and given it to her but pride and a lack of takings stopped me, and so I did the next best thing. I pretended not to care.

I looked up at Paula. She saw me and that made me feel bad and I dropped my eyes and shook my head. Ten minutes later Paula went past me. She was singing, *"we're in the money!"* And clicking her fingers. I didn't look up. I was doing a sudoku but I could picture her face. It was disgusting. I coloured in some sudoku squares. When Paula went past again singing the same song with Enrique in tow I closed my eyes tight. Enrique didn't know the words. He joined in only on the 'money' bit.

"Yeah alright," I said, standing straight when Marcel joined the conga line. He didn't know *any* of the words and was just going. 'rah rah rah.' They didn't stop though, they just danced past me and down the drinks aisle. Took them about one minute and twenty seconds per lap. When Paula eventually appeared by the magazines I smiled to show I was actually a good guy. It was fun, what they were doing, nothing more. We were all having a big load of fun.

"Okay," I faux sighed, "I'm in." But Paula didn't respond. "I'm in!" I shouted, trying to smile.

"Too late!" Shouted Paula. The other two nodded and smiled but I think, I *hope*, they were just caught up in the moment and weren't smiling at my expense. I smiled too. "You stupid fucking cunt!" I shouted then turned to make sure no customers had come in and heard me. None had and when I looked back they were out of sight once more. "Stupid fucking cunt," I said to myself. The dance broke up somewhere towards the back of the shop amid gales of laughter. Marcel went past first. He gave me a thumbs up. Then Enrique appeared mopping his forehead with a hanky.

"I like dat!" He said nodding his head violently. I nodded. "What chu spend chor half on when we win?" He asked.

"I don't even... want... to," I replied and left it hanging. Enrique dried his face thoroughly, still beaming.

When he realised I wasn't adding to that he turned

to Paula and said, "chu get me if you do dat again!" He then looked appreciatively at his hanky and returned to his office.

Before closing time Paula approached me. "Only joking, are you in?" She asked. She seemed genuine.

"Oh that was a great joke," I told her but I was very relieved indeed. I wasn't going to show it but I was very happy. I went for my wallet.

"It was a good joke, you were nearly crying," she said with bright eyes burning like fire. I kept calm, couldn't blow this again.

"Fuck off, was I," I said. Did that make sense? Just. "It's okay," she said. "You in, yeah?"

"I suppose," I told her.

"Suppose?"

"Yeah, I'm in," I said.

"You don't soun-"

"Stick it up your fat arse you fucking..." Luckily for Paula the word I was searching for hasn't even been invented yet. It was a bad one though. Probably would've taken her head off. Paula walked away laughing.

At about 2am I phoned Paula and negotiated a deal in which I also pay her share of the ticket and then I *finally* slept.

24

Samsquanch

It's my own fault, I suppose. I'm a Good Samaritan. The thing with being a Good Samaritan is you get all the shit. I'm not even sure what the upside is. Like, the guy who just walked on past got to go and do what he wanted whereas the Good Samaritan who stops gets his day all fucked up. I'm the good guy who gets his shit fucked up helping fucking idiots. I should be in the Bible.

See, Enrique's had a TV in my garage for quite some time. It's a bit tragic really. He has it set up in the corner and he's put other stuff around it to make it look like a complete home entertainment centre. Under the TV is my old Sky box (no card or power lead), a paint splattered tape recorder and two speakers. None of it works. The TV works but he doesn't have an aerial so it doesn't really work - not in the accepted sense.

The worst thing is when I catch him watching TV through my living room window. I have to get up and draw the curtains.

He had asked me to sort him out with an aerial and I've been ignoring him but yesterday I was bored because my wife was away and I told him I could get him Sky TV for only £50 a month. He was all for that and so I ran the cable from the back of my Sky HD+ box out to his TV. The cable had originally gone up to our bedroom but we never watch telly in bed so for £50 a month it was well worth running it out to the garage instead.

The cabling is a bit of a mess. I've put it under the doormat and out the back door and ran it around some plant pots but I'm going to have to do it properly one day. Get some cable clips for the house. I'll do it when I get a chance. I used the RF2 output on the back of the box.

Anyway, took 20 minutes and Enrique has satellite TV. Of course he can only watch what I'm watching but he won't realise. I told him Sky just shows what it shows and that's half the fun of it.

Last night the phone rings.

"Are you fucking watching this, man!" Said Enrique, breathless.

"Of course I'm watch..." I began. "What are you doing phoning me up?"

"Dey gonna find it, man!" He said ignoring my question.

"They're not going to find it," I told him. I was watching Finding Bigfoot on the Discovery Channel because there was fuck all else on.

"I think dey find it, man," he said. "Show no called No Finding Bigfoot."

"Okay!" I told him putting the phone down. When the phone was halfway down I heard a scream from the handset and so I put it back to my ear. "What?"

"Footprint!" Shouted Enrique. I looked at the TV. A woman was looking at some mud in night vision.

"Listen, I *think* if they'd found Bigfoot it might have been on the news by now," I told him.

There was no response - just heavy breathing - so I did put the phone down. I looked at the TV. I wasn't enjoying the show and watching it with Enrique made it even worse. I turned the channel to Sky Arts and turned off the telly and the living room lights and headed to bed. I was three steps up before guilt got the better of me and I went back and put Finding Bigfoot back on. A split second after I'd put it back on the phone rang one ring and that angered me so much I considered putting Sky Arts back on but, luckily for Enrique, I fought it.

46862638R00100

Made in the USA
Charleston, SC
26 September 2015